BAD BOSSES

The 10 Leadership Pitfalls Followers Most Resent

DAVID SMITH

Grosvenor House
Publishing Limited

This book is published by
Grosvenor House Publishing Ltd
Link House
140 The Broadway, Tolworth, Surrey, KT6 7HT.
www.grosvenorhousepublishing.co.uk

A CIP record for this book
is available from the British Library

ISBN 978-1-78623-661-6

DEDICATION

To my Grandchildren, who bring me constant joy, and keep me young!

CHAPTER 1 INTRODUCTION

What prompted the writing of a 4th book?

> "A bad boss can take good people and 'destroy' them, causing the best people to flee, and the remainder to lose all motivation."
>
> Brigette Hyacinth

News headlines constantly evidence bad bosses

I have felt compelled for a while, to write a 4th book, because of the current climate, in which bosses are doing things which cannot be good for performance or the health of their workforce. I felt that I must say something insightful about the behaviour of bad leaders.

What has caused me to feel this way? I see evidence of poor leadership almost every day; in the press; on television and in business life generally. It prompted me to engage in some research into the subject of the behaviour of bad bosses.

I hope you feel, as the reader, that this is a timely subject.

We have seen the UK Prime Minister step down, due to a total lack of leadership. I'm sure much will be written reflectively about Theresa May as a Prime Minister, much of which will not be kind. Her Election 'campaign' in which she totally lost a storming lead by bad oration and inability to make an inspirational speech, will become legendary.

A 2019 report by the Institute of Leadership and Management has shown that trust in CEOs has fallen by 8% when compared with 2011, after interviews with 800 executives.

The UK's interminable machinations over Brexit, have taken the confidence in Politicians of all parties to an all-time low. Leaders around the world are regularly accused of lies, corruption and deception.

Even the Charity sector, which exists purely to do good, has been exposed to corruption and behaviour of the worst kind. Oxfam has been charged by the Charity Commission with making radical reform, after the cases of sexual exploitation in Haiti, which occurred with survivors after the earthquake there. There were also many other cases of harassment and bullying in Oxfam needing to be addressed. It seems that a swathe of the Charity sector has similar problems.

Google, always previously held up as an exemplar of a good employer, has recently seen employees in London and other locations around the world share personal stories of harassment and discrimination in the workplace. The 2018 walkout of 1000s of Google employees in locations worldwide prompted Sundar Pichai, Google's CEO, to say he would be taking a much harder stance on inappropriate behaviour.

We have witnessed the resignation of Ray Kelvin, ex CEO of the Retailer Ted Baker, and the effect his behaviour had on the share price of that business, not to mention the trauma he had produced amongst former co-workers over many years.

The resignation of Jeff Fairburn, ex CEO of Persimmon Homes, was another expose on the eye watering pay packages some executives are awarding themselves. His annual bonus was a staggering £75million, and the public backlash was so great that it caused his resignation. The amazing thing was that he had no idea how bad this would look, nor did he realise how serious the situation was as the story broke in the media.

Sir Philip Green has been roundly criticised in the news media, particularly over his use of non-Disclosure Agreements to silence employee allegations of bullying and inappropriate behaviour. Sir Philip strenuously denies any wrongdoing, but the effect on his personal wealth and retail estate has been dramatic.

The film industry also has witnessed the fall of giants after the Harvey Weinstein scandal and the subsequent establishment of the #Me Too movement.

These sort of events in recent times, are but a sample of bad leadership behaviour, and the list could go on. You would have hoped that, with the vast lexicon of leadership literature that has been written, and with so many attending leadership programmes and training.....that mankind would have progressed to better leadership in the 21st Century!

However, evidence would suggest that we are experiencing a dearth of truly outstanding leadership. In fact, there are far too many contra examples of bad bosses for anyone to feel that progress is being made.

The behaviour of Bad Bosses has an effect on the well-being of subordinates

We should look at this subject of 'Bad Bosses' from the perspective of employees who are subject to poor behaviour by their leaders.

The UK Health & Safety Executive reported 595,000 workers suffering from work related stress, depression and anxiety in the year 2017/2018. These figures have risen by a whopping 24% per annum, which gives rise to the view that this is a growing problem.

The UK Government has commissioned a report during 2018, looking into the topic of mental health in the workplace. Lord Stevenson of Coddenham, who co-wrote that report, said that not only should bosses be nice to their people, but it is in their economic interests to do so. Good leader behaviour is part of the key to productivity, and bad boss behaviour is the converse.

The report estimates that the cost of poor mental health to the economy, is somewhere in the region of £74billion to £99billion. That is a very sizeable chunk of cash, and some of that mental health cost results from the behaviour of bad bosses. It follows logically that bad boss behaviours are part of the UK's productivity problems. The health, performance and engagement issues that organisations experience, are at least in part, issues which lie at the door of poor leadership.

The attitudes, behaviours and decisions of bad bosses, can cause or exacerbate the problems of workplace stress. A CIPD (Chartered Institute of Personnel and Development) Survey alongside the organisation Simply Health, asked over 1000 HR professionals about the issue of workplace stress. 37% of businesses had experienced workplace stress related illnesses in 2018, and 43% reported that management style was a contributory factor.

Bad bosses cause suffering for their subordinates, but their behaviour also has a financial cost to the organisation. This is not something which should be swept under the carpet!

Command and Control Leadership is alive and well

CEOs regularly tell me that their businesses are run largely in a 'command and control' style, and I observe that 'modus operandi' in too many workplaces. The only conclusion that I can form, is that the autocratic style of command and control, is still alive and well in the 21st century.

This is despite the fact that a command and control style rarely produces good results. In fact, the only time an autocratic style produces optimum results is in a crisis. At a time of crisis, most subordinates will turn to the boss, and look to their leader to make a definitive pronouncement. Equally, in crisis, they are much more likely to do exactly what the leader has prescribed.

However, we don't live in perpetual crisis, and in normal circumstances this is very much a sub-optimal way of going about leadership. Commonly, command and control leaders in normal times will serve to demotivate and demoralise the workforce. They will feel their contribution is ignored, and this will contribute to poor workforce productivity.

I made a search of common leadership styles, and came up with 4 models in modern parlance. There is a 7 factor model/a 6 factor model/a 4 factor model/ and a 3 factor model. You will notice 2 common factors as I summarise these for you:-

7 Styles of Leadership:

- Democratic Leadership – commonly effective
- Autocratic Leadership – rarely effective
- Laissez Faire Leadership – sometimes effective
- Strategic Leadership – commonly effective
- Transformational Leadership – sometimes effective
- Transactional Leadership – sometimes effective
- Bureaucratic Leadership – rarely effective

Please note that, as I have already pointed out, autocratic leadership is rarely effective.

6 Styles of Leadership:

- Visionary – mobilise toward a vision
- Coaching – develop people for the future
- Affiliative – create emotional bonds
- Democratic – build a consensus
- Pace Setting – expect excellent self-direction
- Commanding – demand immediate compliance

The commonality between these 2 models are the styles of Democratic and Commanding leadership. This pattern will continue.

4 Styles of Leadership:

- Autocratic/Authoritarian
- Democratic/Participative
- Laissez Faire/Free rein
- Paternalistic

Again, with only 4 defined styles – autocratic and democratic still appear in the factors.

3 Styles of Leadership:

- Authoritarian – rule over everyone
- Democratic – include everyone
- Laissez Faire – leave it to function

Even with only 3 styles/factors defined, our two constants Authoritarian and Democratic appear again.

The reader will take careful note that although these definitions of styles of leadership vary in number and description, a command and control/authoritarian or autocratic style is defined in every single model. Despite the fact that this sort of style is antiquated for the modern world, and rarely works (except in extremis) it still exists today. Autocratic styles stifle creativity and kill motivation, but bad bosses are still deploying this sort of method of leading.

I think we would all agree that great leaders can massively enhance the output of their people by their behaviour. Conversely, it is true also to say that bad bosses can hugely reduce effort by behaving in the wrong way.

UK productivity is a very topical concern, and the bad bosses out there must bear some of the responsibility for that.

Bad Bosses drive (unplanned) high labour turnover

When I was the People Director of Asda Stores, I was constantly being told (on the basis of the results of exit interviews held with leavers from the business) that our number one issue was the rate of pay. "People are leaving us for more money David," was the common cry from line managers. The Asda business of the early 1990's was in so much financial difficulty, that there was no money available to address any pay disparity with the market. However, instinctively, I didn't believe that was the fundamental problem. I just didn't accept what the exit interviews were feeding back. People resigning usually look for an 'easy' conversation with their supervisor or boss, when tendering their notice to leave. They are prone to telling you that they have found another job, which pays them a little more. It's a very easy conversation to have, in a tricky situation, and avoids any potential conflicts.

Most employees find it difficult face to face to tell their boss that they began looking for another job because of the bad behaviour of that very leader.

We stopped conducting exit interviews during my time at Asda, because they were a complete waste of time. They gave no useful data, and were not getting to the heart of the issue. We replaced exit interviews with a leavers' questionnaire – sent out 6 months after individuals had left the business. We were surprised by the return rate, obviously individuals had settled elsewhere and were happy to comment. The response rate was around 50% of those surveyed. We merely gave them a list of 50 potential reasons why they might have begun looking for a new role, and asked them to tick any factors in the list which applied to them. The results were extremely useful.

People were not in fact primarily leaving because of pay disparities (as reported from the previous exit interviews). The top reason for leaving was poor management style, closely followed by a shift rota which just didn't fit their family circumstances. Pay disparity came well down the list.

It is my experience from Asda, and many other businesses elsewhere, that people don't leave companies. They actually leave the person they are working for. If that relationship is right, they are much harder to 'lure' away. Connectivity to the boss is 'sticky' if that relationship is good.

I was recently looking at a list from an industry/ commerce wide study, giving the top reasons why people leave companies. Interestingly, this correlates directly with my Asda experience, and my knowledge of business generally:

The 7 reasons why employees leave

- Loss of trust in leaders
- Lack of coaching/feedback
- No growth/job opportunity
- Lack of motivation/recognition
- The job/workplace didn't meet expectations
- Mismatch of job to person
- Stress/work life balance

Firstly, pay is not mentioned in those top 7 reasons for leaving. Pay comes in as a secondary consideration. It is not the starter reasons for looking.

You will note that the number one issue here is the behaviour of the leaders. If you lose trust in your boss, that is a killer issue. It is bad bosses who drive people to leave! Their poor leadership habits commence people looking for another job elsewhere. Their lack of feedback to their people. Their failure to recognise outstanding work, and motivate the troops. These are the issues which cause churn of talent.

The cost of hiring and training new people, is a significant expense in any business or organisation. The last thing any enterprise needs, is leadership behaviour by bad bosses which drives your very best people out of the door. By definition, it is always the best people (those who can) who get another job. Only those who are stuck will remain. What an indictment for the bad bosses that they keep the worst people!!

What to do about the problem of bad bosses?

My reason for writing this book, is to address the issue of bad leadership. What does it look like, and what are the things bad bosses do which most demotivate their followers?

So much has been written about leadership generally, and how best to lead, that you would have expected that humankind would have made more progress in becoming good leaders! It's not as if no one knows what good leadership looks like.

My perception, observing politics; business; the charity sector and other spheres, is that we are suffering from a dearth of truly great leadership. Followers are suffering from many of the worst traits that bad bosses can exhibit.

I decided to set about researching the topic of '"what most irritates followers in leadership behaviour?" Some of my results will not surprise you, but others may shock you as the reader. More of this in chapter 2.

SUMMARY POINTS:

- There is evidence of bad leadership in all walks of life – we see bad bosses and their behaviour in the news media almost daily.

- Bad Bosses affect the health and wellbeing of employees negatively, and this is a direct cost to the businesses they work in plus the economy overall.

- Bad bosses are responsible for a proportion of the mental health issues in the workforce.

- People leave bad bosses, rather than Companies.

- Bad leadership drives employee turnover, yet is often hidden as a factor in exit interview data.

- Command and control as a leadership style is outdated – yet it is alive and well in 21st century organisations.

- Bad bosses are one of the factors in poor productivity and business output.

YOUR ACTION:

Are you concerned about any leadership behaviours – either in yourself or those who work directly to you? Might this be affecting the well-being or performance of your people? Would you know this was happening?

CHAPTER 2 MY RESEARCH INTO THE LEADER BEHAVIOURS WHICH MOST IRRITATE FOLLOWERS

In order to understand, first we must listen to those who have been led by bad bosses

> "Hundreds of books and millions of dollars in consulting fees have been devoted to leadership and organisational change. The most important things a leader can bring to a changing organisation are passion, conviction and confidence in others. Leaders set the direction, define the context and help produce coherence for their organisations."
>
> Rosabeth Moss Kanter
>
> "I wonder if there is anyone in the world who can really direct the affairs of the world, or of his country, with any assurance of the results his actions would have?"
>
> Montagu C Norman

Willing volunteers to share stories of bad bosses

When I explained the purpose of my research – to understand the most irritating behaviour that leaders can exhibit – to CEOs and a variety of other Executives, everyone was ready with a story to tell!! Many said that they could fill my book themselves. Other began with the words "let me tell you about a bad boss who….."

I wanted to compile a list of the top 'what not to do's' if you are a leader. I have found no lack of volunteers with stories about their pet hates in leader behaviour. From this research, it was always my intention to compile the top 10 things a leader should avoid doing.

Too much past research has emphasised what great leaders should do

My contention is that too much has been written over the years, about what the ideal leader should do. There has not been sufficient emphasis on what not to do. There are some really corrosive pitfalls that the budding leader should not fall into. Knowing what really irritates and demotivates followers must have real value!

I believe this research and the subsequent 'don't do' list will be both powerful and cathartic for leaders, and you as the reader.

The work of Morgan McCall and Michael Lombardo – 10 Fatal flaws of failed top executives

My search of previous writing on this topic, revealed the work of McCall and Lombardo, from back in the early 1990's. They came up with a list of 10 fatal flaws of failed top executives:-

- Insensitivity to others; abrasive; intimidating; bullying style (that felt like 2 or 3 flaws rolled into one to me!).
- Coldness; aloofness; arrogance.
- Betrayal of trust.
- Excessive ambition; tendency to think of the next job; playing 'politics'.
- Specific performance problems with the business.
- Over-management; inability to delegate/build teams.
- Inability to staff effectively.
- Inability to adapt to a boss with a different style.
- Excessive dependence on an advocate or mentor.

My feeling was that this was a good list in parts, but that it was 30 years out of date. Some of the points raised by McCall and Lombardo were more powerful than others, and a few were quite woolly and didn't resonate for me.

I felt the need to take the mood of followers and leaders of today, in the 21st century.

The essence of my research

I have spoken with almost 200 CEOs, and other executives, on this topic of bad boss behaviours.

I asked them for their worst horror story. Some of these will appear (suitably anonymised for the protection of both the innocent and the guilty!!) in the chapters of this book.

The examples given were often dramatic, certainly vividly remembered, and always heartfelt. Frequently, the kind of bad boss behaviour resulted in resignations from the company (as I have already stated – people leave bosses rather than companies) or began the intent to leave later when the timing was right.

In every case, even when bad leadership behaviour didn't drive departure from the organisation, subordinates expressed feelings of demotivation, frustration and a resulting reduction in the discretionary effort they were prepared to give.

Leadership behaviour matters! Bad boss behaviour is corrosive. It is counter to creating a good culture, and ultimately will kill performance in followers. Yet despite the fact that we all know this, there appears to be a wealth of horror stories emanating from the bad bosses out there in the real world.

My research revealed some bad behaviours, which didn't make the top 10 most frequently mentioned. They are still clearly relevant, because they came up in my research, but haven't the frequency to hit my top 10 worst behaviours. I have dedicated the next chapter to mention those irritants, since I think they are still worthy of mention. If you find yourself 'guilty as charged' with perpetrating any of these behaviours (or you see them in other leaders in your business), then I believe they still warrant attention. It is worth thinking about how you might modify your own behaviour as a leader, or that of your own top team.

My research certainly identified a top 10 list of the leadership pitfalls, which most irritate followers. I have listed the top 10 in order of frequency of mention, so as to give you an ascending order of magnitude. The top 10 are clearly the worst exhibits of demotivating bad boss behaviour. I will dedicate a chapter of this book to each of the top 10 leadership pitfalls which most irritate, and the order will build according to their frequency of mention by followers. I don't attempt to rank the seriousness of these pitfalls, merely to highlight that frequency of mention builds from number 10 to number 1.

As a leader, reading this book, your job is to ensure that none of these things is happening in your own organisation, on your watch. This may not necessarily be a concern about your own personal behaviour, but it may be the behaviours of members of your leadership team.

Organisations need to monitor/measure and manage leadership behaviours. Executives need to be held to company values and standards of behaviour. They should recognise that failure to do so will degrade the wellbeing and performance of their teams – and be a source of unwanted churn of talent.

<u>What will you do with the research results?</u>

I guess the 'nub' of the issue, as you read this book, is what you will do with the output of this research?

Will you assume that none of this applies to you or your team leaders? Or will you engage in measuring leadership behaviours amongst yourself and your leadership teams? Will you give the teams in your organisation the opportunity to give anonymous feedback to yourself and their leaders?

My experience, over 35 years of corporate life, and many more since, has taught me that all bosses have a tendency to think themselves better leaders than they are.

Anonymous feedback from your followers, telling you how you come across as a leader to them, has to be invaluable. It is only by measuring, and taking action, on subordinate feedback, that we can improve our leadership behaviours. It is vitally important to deal with those things in our own behaviour, or the behaviours of our leadership teams, which most irritate or demotivate our followers.

It is my view that many leaders fail to calculate just how much the behaviour of bad bosses (at various levels in the organisation) is 'killing' or downgrading the company culture. Actions which downgrade company culture will damage overall performance. Having the title manager or director does not give any person the right to behave in any way that they like. We all need to be responsible for 'rooting out' the sort of behaviours that most irritate followers. We should be growing a strong, healthy high performance culture – not behaving in a way that switches off the best efforts of our people.

SUMMARY POINTS:

- There is a wealth of stories from people about the bad bosses they have worked for.
- Memories of bad boss behaviour are both vivid and corrosive in effect.
- Much of the leadership literature has stressed how to be a good leader – rather than to identify the serious leadership pitfalls to be avoided at all costs.
- There is a need for an up to date analysis of the current frustrations in the workplace about the behaviour of bad bosses.
- Leaders need to determine to measure, and act upon, leadership behaviours in any organisation which fall below the values and norms that have been established.
- The way leaders behave is a bellwether of culture, and has a direct bearing on performance.

YOUR ACTION:

Will you commit to the measurement, and feedback to leaders on their behaviour, from the perspective of employees in your own organisation?

CHAPTER 3 SOME IRRITATIONS ABOUT BAD BOSSES WHICH DIDN'T MAKE THE TOP 10 LIST

The research findings may surprise you

> "A good leader, who treats people well and always develops a great culture, will make a business thrive. A selfish leader, who doesn't understand people, will cause a company to crumble."
>
> Richard Branson
>
> "We cannot ask others to do what we have not done ourselves."
>
> Christiana Figueres

My personal expectations of what I might discover

I had some expectations about the kind of things people might say about the bad bosses they had experienced.

I was aware of the research at Harvard Business School concerning the inclusiveness of bosses. In the modern environment of the 21st century, teams comprise diverse capabilities; backgrounds and generational groupings. If all team members in an organisation are treated respectfully, and are valued fairly – giving them a real sense of belonging – then they are more likely to feel confident and inspired. Harvard research has shown that teams managed in that inclusive management style, make better quality decisions; work more collaboratively and produce better performance.

<u>My list of expected leadership failings before research</u>

My own view was that there would be some failings of bosses which would come out on top of the list of those executives I was about to survey. I guess anyone who has worked for a boss would have some pre-conceived notions of what most irritates followers.

My personal list, before I began to interview people, was as follows:-

i. <u>Failure to focus on an overarching purpose</u>
   My view is that employees need something to rally around. There has to be a belief that your work is contributing to more than just making money – however important that may be.

ii. <u>The inability to inspire followers</u>
   I'm personally convinced that the power of inspirational communication to motivate followers is mission critical for any leader. Those who cannot do this commit a major 'faux par' in my book. I've seen too many leaders who have an over reliance on email, and don't have an inspirational bone in their body. In my view, it was one of the prime reasons for failure in Theresa May as UK Prime Minister.

iii. Failure to bring pace and external ideas in
Leaders who are not driven themselves find it hard to drive performance. Leaders who do not spend a proportion of their time making external contacts miss the trends, and don't bring new ideas into the business. I would not follow a leader who didn't bring real energy, and an external orientation.

iv. Leaders who just don't care about people
Some people just use other people. For them, employees are a commodity. It's a sad fact of life. They neither want to associate or affiliate with their people. For them, labour is there to be utilised. No matter what is done by the followers, nothing will be appreciated by this type of boss. They are the kind who cause major burnout in the people who work for them. I don't rate people 'users', and couldn't work for one.

v. Failure to decide – leaders with analysis paralysis
I've witnessed organisations and executives agonising over conflicting data. In real life, you never know all the answers and all the variables. Requesting yet more data, and giving more deliberation doesn't help. Leading is about making judgement calls, based upon the information available. You have to make a call as a leader, and trial some things to see how they work. You cannot mitigate all risks. Followers want their bosses to take calculated risks. They loathe a leader who is a permanent ditherer.

vi. Failure to live the declared values of the business
When a top team have defined the way the people in the business should behave, I personally detest executives who think those rules don't apply to them. They seem to feel they are above 'all that values stuff' because they are too senior! I've worked alongside a few, and we inevitably clashed over this principle. I think it's a big no-no for followers generally.

vii. Leaders whose behaviour is inappropriate
I've seen heavy drinkers (who were otherwise perfectly capable) lose the respect of their colleagues. I've witnessed the effect on followers of executives constantly using excessive bad language. Some senior executives behave as sexual pariahs, and that drives people out of an organisation if it is not stopped quickly. Bad boss behaviour takes many forms, from bullying to harassment, and being in a position of power does not entitle the boss to behave badly.

That was my own list of the top irritations, and my research interviews revealed that some of this seven things irritate other followers too. However, not all my own guesses were correct.

This book is not about what I might think are the worst bad boss behaviours, but about what my research revealed. This chapter will go on to reveal some of the irritating behaviours of bad bosses which didn't make the top 10 pitfalls list.

Leaders who don't do what they say they will do

Firstly, followers were irritated by leaders who didn't keep to their word.

When I worked for Asda Stores, we had a little acrostic, which I like very much, and have never forgotten. DWYSWYD; which stood for 'do what you say you will do'. Leaders who do this regularly, get a powerful positive response from their followers. Being a person of your words matters in leadership. Not adhering to this is a powerful negative turn off.

Followers told me that they didn't respect bosses who didn't do what they said they would do, and when they said they would do it.

It seems to me, that in life generally (and certainly in the workplace) you can rely on some people who always do what they say they will do. I know many people, who when they say something will be done, I mentally tick it off as completed. With other people, I know there will be no chance. People give their respect and extra discretionary effort to those leaders who are people of their word.

This irritant didn't make the top 10, but it is certainly one to watch if you are a leader of others.

Bosses who fail to delegate and micro manage

Poor leaders never know when to 'pass the baton'. The organisation fails to win races, because not everyone is allowed to play their part in the right timescale.

Some bosses try to control all the work personally, rather than 'handing on' to reliable members of their teams. Their whole mind set is that of 'rescuer' or 'control freak', rather than effective leader. Such bosses may think they are helping out by micro managing projects, but their followers do not feel the same way. Telling people what to do, and how and when may be helpful to a new beginner, but for everyone else I surveyed, they wanted their leaders to step back and let them do their bit.

Micromanaging competent teams kills initiative and effort. My research showed that over time, the result will be that followers stop using their initiative and their brain at work, because they knew that the boss would dictate the pace. I'm sure this is a familiar 'doom loop' which many readers will have seen or experienced. It may not have made the top 10, but is a 'watch out' for bosses everywhere.

Bosses who fall down on execution

Some bosses have a 'butterfly brain'. They flit from one thing to another. Bad bosses are obsessed by the latest and newest thing they come across. They are initiators but not completers. Failure in the business to finish anything well ensues. My respondents talked about being left confused by what the boss was looking for, and what needed to be prioritised. In those circumstances, great execution was the casualty.

Execution by the organisation of key tasks can never be brilliant if the leader gives muddled messages. I wonder how many poor executors you have worked with in your own career? This didn't make the top 10 irritants, but certainly featured in my research.

Bad bosses are issue/conflict avoidist

Some of my respondents talked about leaders they had worked for, who irritated them by not facing a looming issue in the business. This might be people performance or market/technical or customer issues.

Part of having a higher pay grade means that you shouldn't avoid a problem or issue that is looming. You cannot be seen to disappear out of the way when a decision is required. My feedback revealed that is exactly what some bosses do.

One story I was told, concerned a Finance Director of a company. He had been made aware of some serious financial issues looming, yet took no action whatsoever. He cleared his desk quietly, one Sunday afternoon when no one was around and disappeared from the company altogether. His role as FD was to take action/to galvanise others, and to flag issues to the CEO. He did none of those things and ran from them.

I have been told about a few such bad bosses, who have gone absent on sick leave, at the height of a major crisis in their businesses. It seems incredible, that some executives run away from trouble, but that is the reaction in some situations. Clearly, there is no credibility with followers for the runaway boss.

Bad bosses who succumb to corruption

My survey revealed that followers cannot tolerate bosses who tell lies and cover up. Deceit has never been an attractive personal trait, but leaders in organisations who go down this path tend to be found out, and subsequently lose all credibility.

Bosses found to be 'on the fiddle' should expect all credibility with followers to be gone. This does not happen sufficiently frequently to make the top 10 pitfalls, but when it does, it is terminal for the career of that executive in that business.

Bosses who spend time generating stress in followers

Stress is an interesting topic. Some stress is natural, and makes us perform to our peak performance. Too much stress is harmful to our wellbeing, and will cause both underperformance and mistakes to be made.

My respondents talked about some bad bosses they had worked for, who deliberately set goals that they knew to be over stretching, and also wilfully took away the resources required for the delivery of those objectives. Such bad bosses were seen as setting people up to fail, rather than setting people up to succeed.

A leader who causes followers to feel over-stretched and stressed by the workload, will not achieve great results. Are you a great leader who sets people up for success, or do you consciously over stretch people, in the belief you will get more from them?

<u>Bosses who are remote and fail to lead from the front</u>

I had some feedback in my research, concerning bosses who don't get out and about in the business. Consequently, these sort of bosses fail to see and know what is really happening. Good executives are always close to the operation and know what is going on. They get feedback on what is happening. Bad bosses don't put in the effort, or take the time to do this. Bad bosses don't walk the talk, and followers tend to despise them because they don't lead by example.

Leading by your position power may have worked 100 years ago, but it certainly doesn't 'cut the mustard' with followers today. A leader cannot expect people to do the things they would not do themselves. Being prepared to 'walk a mile' with the workforce, goes a long way in achieving credibility.

How close are you to the 'pulse' of your organisation and its people?

<u>Bad bosses fail to manage change effectively</u>

A number of my respondents mentioned this feature. Some leaders they had worked for were not change managers. Their preference was for the status quo. They operated in their own 'comfort zone', with the things they found familiar. Bad bosses they talked about tended to do things how they had always been done, using what they had always known.

We know this type of behaviour is dangerous, because we live in a fast changing world. Success comes to leaders who can harness change, and can get their organisation changing at a speed appropriate to their market, and ahead of their competition. Many bad bosses failed to realise the change needed, and didn't have the courage or determination to drive any change. Even those who saw the need for change, didn't seem to have the capability to drive it. Followers found this to be unacceptable behaviour, but it exists, and has been the prime reason for failure in many businesses.

Change can be unpopular initially, and weak leaders are often diverted by negative feedback. Change leaders need to be able to spot what is required, and to drive it through. Are you a change leader, or do you occasionally feel like that rabbit 'caught frozen' in the car headlights? Followers want action from leaders.

Bad bosses tend to be far too 'short termist'

I had a number of respondents talk to me about the need for bosses who have a longer term vision beyond next quarter's profit figure.

Failure to lead with a longer term agenda, is not a good indicator for followers. Having a BHAG ('big hairy audacious goal') is the kind of thing followers will tend to respond to.

One of my interviewees spoke about working for a CEO who decided to increase 1000 prices in retail stores, in order to meet his short term profit objective. He was strongly advised that this was a bad idea by his leadership team, but he pressed ahead anyway. The teams in the retail stores were flooded with price change activity, and this also caused customers to leave their shop with part filled trolleys of goods. The business lost all credibility with its customers, and the Board lost all credibility with the retail employees in the stores. No one trusted that particular CEO ever again.

We all need to beware of responding to short term targets, which will do longer term harm. Better to miss a short term target, for the sake of the longer term game. 'Short termism' is a credibility killer with followers.

This topic didn't make the top 10 of pitfalls, but it is one I see reported in the press frequently. Beware short termism!

Bad bosses are inconsistent

The final piece of my research which didn't make the top 10 pitfalls, was this topic of inconsistency.

Leaders who are 'all over the place' in their reactions to events, fail to realise that followers respond best to clear and consistent direction. Bosses shouldn't be mercurial. Some of my interviews revealed that bad bosses change more often that the British weather.

I was told a story about a high performing employee who worked for a family firm. She began looking for another job elsewhere, not because of any under-performance issues, but because someone else (who was a performer) had been 'let go' to make way for a family member. She didn't know when or if she might be next, at the vagaries of the family.

Inconsistencies by leaders kill performance in followers, and ultimately may be a cause for unwanted churn of talent.

Irritations in followers are corrosive to performance

Most of the issues that came up in my research, which I have just articulated, were not frequently raised. Hence they have not made the top 10 leadership pitfalls. However, if these type of behaviours occur in your own working situation – they are productivity and morale killers.

There is no such thing as a minor issue here. Bad bosses who exhibit these behaviours, can expect them to influence performance negatively, to varying degrees.

I guess that most bosses don't come to work each day plotting how they can ruin the lives of subordinates. I'm equally sure they don't attend work looking to sabotage performance. Being aware of the behaviour which irritate followers, is half the battle to avoiding such leadership pitfalls. I trust that the realisation that these things happen out there in the real world, will cause you to seek to stamp them out in your own business.

Ask around amongst employees. Do they see any of this kind of thing happening? Keep yourself informed. Walk the talk with your people. You may be surprised by what they are prepared to tell you!

SUMMARY POINTS:

- We all probably have a mental list of the leadership failings we think are the worst.
- Leaders who don't do what they say they will do, are bound to cause irritation amongst followers.
- Bosses who over-manage and fail to delegate, will never get the best from their team(s).
- Muddled messages and a butterfly brain are a sure-fire recipe for poor execution. Be a completer.
- Bad bosses avoid responsibility and accountability. Don't be a runner from trouble.
- If you succumb to corruption as a leader, your reputation with your people is finished.
- Bad bosses deliberately or inadvertently cause stress amongst the workforce. Stressed people either burn out, or certainly can't produce their best work.
- Bad bosses fail to be effective change leaders. They are remote, and can't lead from the front.
- Bad bosses are blown about by short termism, and are consistently inconsistent.

YOUR ACTION:

These traits in chapter 3 have not made the top 10 pitfalls, but they are still serious, and merit serious consideration by any leader wanting a high performance culture. They need to be spotted when they occur, and action needs to be taken to prevent recurrence/curb behaviour, or in extreme cases remove offending executives from the business.

Do you recognise any of these traits in either yourself or managers in your teams?

CHAPTER 4 FAVOURITISM

Bad bosses can be very unfair to others

"Earn your leadership every day."

Michael Jordan

"A lot of people have gone further than they thought, because someone else thought they could,"

Zig Ziglar

"Don't pick a job, pick a boss! Your first boss is the biggest factor in your career success. A boss who doesn't trust you, won't give you opportunities to grow."

William Raduchel

"The right of commanding is no longer an advantage transmitted by nature; like an inheritance, it is the fruit of labours, the price of courage."

Voltaire

Into the top 10 pitfalls – that lack of 'grit in the Oyster'

The grit in the oyster is the base to form the pearls, so they tell me. It's that objectivity and development which grows great people in the workplace. Talent should be merit based and earned by a combination of ability, graft and nurturing by a coaching boss.

I begin my list of the top 10 irritants for followers which goes against those principles of a meritocracy. That of favouritism. My respondents saw this as a key pitfall of leaders. Whether those favourites are, or are not, relatives of the boss, having favourites who 'can do no wrong' is a characteristic which beguiles many bosses.

So, number 10 in the survey list of pitfalls which followers loathe is having favourites. We all would acknowledge that we have an inbuilt bias when selecting people into an organisation at interview. That is, we tend to like people naturally, who are like us, and hold similar views about the world to our own. Actually, the last person we should bring into the team, is another person like us. This adds nothing to the gene pool of talent or difference. It can also exacerbate 'group think', and a lack of challenge to decision making. Teams need difference. That 'grit' in the oyster, which can produce the pearls of ideas and breakthroughs, is all about harnessing differing views and talents, and a healthy atmosphere of challenge.

My own early job experience of Nepotism

In my early working life, I worked for a good number of years in Britain's then very sizeable Coal Industry. British Coal was a traditional Nationalised heavy industry. The management style predominating was paternalistic, and the hiring and promotion riddled with paternalism.

I spent a fair number of years heading up Training and Development, and many of the young trainees were the sons (no women were allowed down coal mines by Law back then) of senior officials who wanted them to follow in their footsteps. I found that many of these people, who were extremely credible and tough as engineers, had a complete 'blindspot' when it came to their offspring. They would interfere, trying desperately to make excuses or build short cuts to 'pave the way' for their children. It was embarrassing to witness, and reduced their credibility as senior people from my perspective.

I remembered it so acutely, that I vowed at the time never to attempt to ease the path for my own 2 sons later in life. Many joked with me during my time on the Board at Asda Stores, that I must have secured a 'cushy' position for my children. I told them, and I meant it, that my sons would never work in the business that I worked in, on principle. I didn't want it to be said that they only got on because of who their father was. Favouritism and nepotism are corrosive to the reputation of a leader. I'm pleased to say that I have avoided that trap.

Nepotism is common in many walks of life

I have come to realise that nepotism was not just a feature of the long since defunct British Coal. Nepotism pervades every walk of life.

Some children certainly go to work in their family firms. Don't get me wrong, some of these offspring have both aptitude and ability. Some have a great work ethic because they belong to the family, and there is pressure for them to be 'seen to earn' their place in the family firm.

I had one employee 'given' to me at British Coal, much to my disgust at the time (based upon my reluctance to take the offspring of senior people), who turned out to be one of the best people who has ever worked for me in my entire career!

However, in some cases, the reverse is true. Owners of businesses have to face the extremely difficult feedback that the family member is not performing. Removing family members from employment with the business causes untold grief within those families where it happens. I have mentored a few CEOs in those difficult circumstances where they have had to fire brothers/sisters/children or even parents. All are excruciatingly difficult!

My respondents talked at some length about the situations where they had observed favouritism or nepotism taking place, and it was an irritant for them. It reduced the credibility of the leaders in their eyes.

No doubt you have observed the machinations of politicians in the UK, during the MPs expenses scandal expose. UK MPs had to admit to employing wives, husbands and children, and often overpaid them for fairly low level work.

US Presidents have famously relied upon family members populating roles in the White House, from the Kennedy clan to the current occupants of the Trump family. President Erdogan of Turkey has appointed his son in law as Turkey's Economy Minister. After meetings with a variety of US investors, they reported that his was the worst performance ever of anyone they had seen occupy that role in any country. Not a great accolade!

It is obvious why people try to help family members. They believe they can trust them, and they are a known quantity. However, the credibility of the leader is reduced immediately in the eyes of the onlookers, especially if the person is not up to the job.

<u>Favouritism demotivates people across the organisation</u>

Favouritism is different to nepotism. Nepotism is all about promoting or advancing your own family. Favouritism is exactly what it says. Having obvious favourites amongst employees.

As a leader, if you have an 'inner circle', within your own team, you will alienate the remainder. You are excluding some, and this will inevitably make you blind or deaf to some of the challenge that you need. There is a great temptation to surround yourself with 'yes men or women', when in actual fact, all bosses need to hear contra voices.

Favouritism can also lead to bias or special treatment and excuses for those favourites who are underperforming.

Letting some people off the hook, whilst applying different criteria to others, does not go unobserved by the followers. Everyone in the organisation is watching, and noting what goes on. It is a real organisation wide turn off for motivation.

I wasn't expecting to hear this type of pitfall to get mentioned so widely in my survey interviews. However, respondents felt very strongly, that unfair treatment across a team, favouring one over others, was a big no-no. This was especially true when it came to development and promotional opportunities.

In some cases, my respondents observed that the source of favouritism was as a result of physical attraction between the two individuals concerned. If the boss was attracted to someone, they would invariably gloss over their inexperience or shortcomings. Such situations, they reported, were very difficult to raise or discuss with the leaders concerned. How do you say to the boss, "you only promoted x because you're attracted to them."

The general consensus of my survey respondents was that employment of friends, almost always caused unfair treatment, and resulted in job underperformance. Objectivity seemed to go out of the window, even where the boss was previously a good judge of performance and behaviour in others.

Working for a boss who favours some rather than you, caused my respondents to express feelings of frustration and helplessness. Not something a leader should be perpetuating in the organisation. It can sometimes be blindness that the boss is being 'played' by those who constantly flatter them in order to get on. Leaders should be harnessing the motivation of all their people, not a 'favoured' few. They should also be capable of spotting those who are 'playing them.'

The ultimate pitfall – the Peter Principle'

Favourites cloud the judgement of a leader. In the same way that our natural biases cause us to hire people that we like, rather than the best person for the job (whether they are like us or not). Similarly, our favouritism can drive us to promote those who are our favourites, and see them as better able to perform a higher role than is the case.

That over confidence in the abilities and potential of certain people can result in some bosses continuing to sponsor and promote people up the levels of an organisation to their 'level of incompetence.' In other words, that boss is guilty of pushing their favourite, over others more capable or suitable, until they actually completely fail in the next job. This is called the 'Peter principle.'

Many respondents to my survey quoted situations where leader sponsored favourites had failed in the job roles to which they had been promoted. This is a leadership pitfall, with major consequences. The consequence for the favourite themselves, is a loss of job role or demotion, and certainly a career car crash. The consequence for the leader is equally serious. They lose all credibility as a boss, and as a talent selector. Credibility is one of those life commodities which takes years to build, but which can be lost in a moment in these sort of circumstances. It is certainly a precious thing which leaders should not throw away lightly.

As a leader yourself reader – don't fall into the favourite trap. It's beguiling, but extremely dangerous territory. Your personal hard earnt credibility is on the line.

SUMMARY POINTS:

- Recognise that we all have inbuilt bias, to like the people in the workplace, who are most like us.

- In all walks of life, there is evidence of business and political figures attempting to help/shelter and provide a career for their family members.

- Nepotism is rife, and can often backfire spectacularly. Onlookers almost never approve, and more often resent such practices.

- Favouritism is divisive; switches off the efforts of the 'out' group, and reduces necessary input and challenge to the leader. It is a source of underperformance and demotivation for followers.

- Realise the favouritism 'trap' puts your own leadership credibility on the line. Credibility in a leader takes time to nurture and grow. It can be lost in a moment, and favouritism is one of the pitfalls where you can lose it.

YOUR ACTION:

Do you have favourites in your own team? Is this one of your credibility danger points?

What action do you need to take to mitigate this?

CHAPTER 5 INDISCRETION/ GOSSIPING

The temptation for idle talk is strong

> "Leaders think and talk about the solutions. Followers think and talk about the problems."
>
> Brian Tracy
>
> "Tend to the people, and they will tend to the business."
>
> John Maxwell
>
> "You manage things; you lead people."
>
> Admiral Grace Murray Hopper

Number 9 Pitfall – 'Loose talk'

'Careless talk costs lives', was a propaganda campaign by the British Government in the Second World War. It was designed to discourage people from talking about any sensitive military or other material which could be overheard by spies in the country. The UK Government also wanted to limit the effect of any morale sapping rumours. The campaign began in 1942, and posters were issued to all ranks of the military, with the best known of those poster images showing people giving away secrets in everyday situations (such as riding on a bus).

Loose talk applies to business situations today, not just to wartime. It is certainly an irritant strongly mentioned by my survey respondents.

Everyone loves a juicy bit of gossip

If we are honest, we wouldn't be human if we didn't admit to deriving some enjoyment from hearing a juicy piece of gossip about a work colleague or situation. Life, in all workplaces, has a 'grapevine'. That informal passing around of information between colleagues happens naturally, and at speed.

In the modern era it has speeded up even more, because it is no longer just verbal, it now also happens via social media. Many a famous person, or sports personality has 'binned' their whole career by one moment of indiscretion.

The actor Liam Neeson must regret his unguarded comment at a press junket, and I'm sure we could all think of other famous people who have had such 'moments'. Loose talk for them has been very expensive indeed. The politician Gordon Brown's reputation as UK Prime Minister was tarnished by having a microphone attached to his lapel during an in car conversation about "that bigoted woman' who was a lifelong Labour Party supporter.

What all leaders need to remember, is that when you are in a leadership position, you have to be the one who rises to a higher personal standard. Followers do not expect their boss to be indiscreet. Being a leader who gossips will only kill your reputation, and dent the morale of your people.

The story of the inebriated CEO

One of my survey respondents told me about their CEO, who was attending an external Industry Awards ceremony, along with her Board team. She talked only to her number 2 all evening (and was therefore also exhibiting pitfall number 10: favouritism), and proceeded to drink way too much during the event.

This CEO became noticeably loud as the evening wore on. She 'slagged off' her own organisation, in an increasingly loud voice, to the ultimate embarrassment of her board team, and others external to the organisation.

Indiscretions of this sort are often 'jarring' for the hearers, and consequently are both damaging, and memorable for all the wrong reasons. Reputation is difficult to rebuild, but so very easy to destroy. The motto for this CEO would be that mixing drink and social occasions were a serious problem, and should have been taken in serious moderation only. They were a catalyst to her reputational downfall.

Gerald Ratner – the 'ultimate' indiscretion

Speaking of indiscretions at official functions. The Company Chairman of Ratners – Gerald Ratner – was speaking at a public event on behalf of the business. No doubt the organisers had asked him to be witty, and make a lively speech. He was trying to lighten the mood by telling a joke against himself, which was subsequently taken out of context. He described a decanter set, sold by Ratner Group, as 'total crap'.

This famous indiscretion has become legendary. It accelerated into a spiral of decline for Britain's then biggest jewellery group, plunging it into the red, and forcing a mass closure programme. Gerald Ratner's life was thrown into complete turmoil, and he quickly went from a luxury champagne lifestyle, to being unemployable, in short order!

I've heard Gerald Ratner speak, in very humble terms, about his indiscretion, and his life story since. He lost it all, and then had a considerably hard time trying to rebuild. The moral of this salutary tale is – be very, very careful what you say. The tongue is a powerful member of the body, and leaders need to take great care how they use it.

The CEO spreading discord in the organisation

Another of my respondents told me the story of one CEO who deliberately said different things to various people in the organisation about senior leaders. He also agreed with different people, even to the extent that he seemed to agree with the very last person who had spoken with him. That particular criticism has certainly been levelled at President Trump!

Whether he had a tactic of deliberately causing tension or not, he certainly caused a lot of confusion by his behaviour. His subordinates weren't ever sure what he really thought, nor what result he really wanted.

The feeling that this CEOs team was left with, was one of total discord. No one was 'on the same page', because the CEO exhibited this gossipy style of management, which resulted in total confusion. The function of good leaders is to get the organisation to consensus, through challenge and debate. Leaders should not 'sow discord', whether by intent or by accident.

The story of the CEO wanting to sell his business

Business deals are exciting. There is always a lot at stake. A deal of detailed work has to go on behind the scenes before things can go public. It is one of those circumstances were leaders cannot communicate, or the deal may evaporate. Indiscretion and gossip are the very last ingredients that a business needs in this very heady mix of circumstances.

Gossipy bosses are naturally leaky. They seem to have a desperate need to talk about things. There are unfortunate consequences to this sort of bad boss behaviour. I was told by one of those surveyed, about a CEO who wanted to sell his business. He talked openly about it with people inside the business, who shouldn't have been involved at that stage, and for whom such matters were well above their pay grade. Dangerous behaviour!

He also talked to a number of people outside the business. So much so, that the rumour mill began to run externally, with commentary in the industry press, and the local newspaper.

In the end, whether because of his indiscretions, or a combination of that and other factors – the whole sale fell through. The buyers had taken fright, and no longer wanted to do the deal. Morale in that business collapsed, because expectations were left unfulfilled, and the leaky CEO had to deal with a major problem totally of his own making. His credibility never really recovered, and there were performance problems in the company for a long time afterwards.

The gossip driving talent turnover

Another respondent told me a salutary story, involving a senior leader in an organisation, who was spreading negative feedback around about one of their senior colleagues. Things got so bad for this recipient of the gossip that they asked to be moved out of their role in the organisation.

Unfortunately, not only was that person's career ruined by this gossiper's indiscretion – the gossiper was promoted into the vacancy that their false stories had caused. The CEO at the time, hadn't realised what was really going on, and when he was told that the removed executive had been 'stitched up' by malicious gossip, he refused to believe the feedback.

The consequence of this sequence of events was to drive up management labour turnover in the organisation. People saw and felt the injustice of what had happened. It made them feel insecure in their own positions, that the CEO could be so easily deluded by gossip and indiscretion. Key players looked for roles outside the business, and some very important talent was lost.

If bad bosses destroy trust through indiscretion, and listen to unproven and unfounded gossip, then those uninvolved lose trust and are unsettled. People begin to think 'this could happen to me', and before you realise, there is a brain drain of talent from the organisation.

Indiscretion is damaging to both boss and organisation

I guess few of us will forget the TV clips of Mike Coupe, the J Sainsbury CEO, singing "we're in the money" off camera before a TV interview about the proposed merger of Sainsbury and Asda. His indiscretion did his reputation harm, and the Sainsbury share price very little good.

Leaders need to be careful what they say at all times. Bosses are always under scrutiny, by employees, media and external agencies. I often say to executives that employees are watching everything you do. They know your circumstance, where you go, what you say – and are matching everything to the values of the business. Beware unintended consequences. Gerald Ratner has spent a lifetime regretting one sentence!!

SUMMARY POINTS:

- Careless talk has consequences!!
- People naturally love to hear a juicy piece of gossip.
- Leaders have to be very careful to rise above gossip and indiscretion despite temptation to talk.
- The tongue is very powerful – guard what you say. It is easy to ruin your hard earned reputation.
- Many careers have been ruined in moments of indiscretion. You could ruin your business – don't forget Gerald Ratner.
- You can easily cause confusion and crash morale.
- You can kill trust and cause churn of your best talent.

YOUR ACTION:

Is gossip or indiscretion happening/tolerated amongst your senior leaders? How would you know? Are you guilty personally of indiscretions? This is one to talk about and openly state that it will not be tolerated. Listen to feedback, and don't ignore what you are told – chase it to source.

CHAPTER 6 CLAIMING WORK DONE BY OTHERS AS YOUR OWN

If you lack confidence: this pitfall can be tempting

"Innovation distinguishes between a leader and a follower."

Steve Jobs

"Leadership is the art of giving people a platform for spreading ideas that work."

Seth Godin

"Don't be intimidated by what you don't know. That can be your greatest strength, and ensure that you do things differently from everyone else."

Sara Blakely

"Inexperience is an asset. Embrace it."

Wendy Kopp

"Leaders have the guts to tell you they don't know what's coming next."

Tom Peters

"Go to the people. Live with them. Learn from them. Love them. Start with what they know. Build

> on what they have. But with the best leaders, when the work is done, the task accomplished, the people will say 'we have done this ourselves'."
>
> Lao Tzu

Leadership Pitfall number 8 – stealing the credit

This type of bad boss behaviour is a real 'stinker'. Followers hate it, and the injustice burns for a long time after the event. My respondents felt very strongly about the lack of fairness, when their contribution was stolen by another. I was constantly and sharply reminded by many of those I surveyed, that this really hurts followers in organisations.

A leader who persistently and very publicly takes the credit for what the team has delivered, is quickly discredited, and eventually loathed by that team. The team may say very little about how it makes them feel to the boss, but they will complain to each other, and the resentment will be very strong indeed.

So many CEO respondents told me about people they had worked for, who stole the credit and stole the ideas of their team – claiming these as their own.

I have often heard it said that the best way to get ideas and new initiatives implemented, is to let the boss think it was their idea in the first place. My research would suggest that this is a 'glib' saying. Followers see this kind of bad boss behaviour as recognition or idea theft.

Bad Bosses may steal ideas because they lack courage

I listened to the feedback from those I surveyed, about bosses stealing credit for the work done by others, and began to ponder the psychology behind that kind of action. Why do bad bosses 'steal' the ideas or work done by others, and claim them as their own?

Clearly, such bosses are insecure in their own position. They feel desperate to prove their worth to superiors above them. Unless they are seen to be achieving results, they must feel exposed to losing credibility, and ultimately their position in the organisation. These sort of bosses don't realise that, by giving credit to members of their teams, it will actually reflect well on them. They will be seen as good leaders who develop and recognise their people. In turn, their people will be highly motivated for being given appropriate credit for their work, and will seek to do more outstanding work. This is a virtuous circle which benefits everyone, and increases productivity.

The bad boss is so desperate to cling onto any good news, they grab achievements to themselves, and close down the efforts of their subordinates. This is a doom loop, which reduces productivity, and makes work miserable.

Good bosses - by comparison - show courage

When Indra Nooyi took over as CEO of PepsiCo in 2006, she noticed a shift in consumer attitudes toward healthier food and drinks. Despite the fact that arch rivals Coca Cola were not following these trends, Indra Nooyi focussed her teams on the pursuit of healthy snacks and drinks.

Indra was challenged in her strategy by an influential activist investor, who wanted her to split the company – but she stoically 'stuck to her guns', and didn't change strategy or direction. As a result of her leadership courage; PepsiCo consistently outperformed Coca Cola. She was a courageous leader, prepared to swim upstream against known industry norms. She is also famous for recognising the outperformance of the people in her organisation. She obsessively sent all recognition letters to the home address of the achiever, so that the whole family would know what had been achieved. Indra understood the virtuous circle, and showed the traits of good bosses.

Many bosses do not have this sort of leadership courage. They focus too much on hitting short term profit targets. They avoid making risky decisions at all costs. They don't want to be seen to 'rock the boat'. These bad bosses don't want to make calls that might make them look at risk to peers and external critics. Such bad bosses regularly put off major decisions, because of their fear of failure.

A poignant story of ideas stolen by a bad boss

One of my respondents talked to me, with a great deal of indignation, about a situation he had witnessed in his open plan office. He was sitting at his work station, opposite the Director of his Department, listening him discussing products which he thought the business should be investing in and developing for future growth. This Director was enthusiastically describing to some fellow Directors, how these products could improve the productivity and profitability of the business. To his amazement, my respondent realised, as this discussion unfolded, that these were the very product ideas which he had put forward to this Director not many days previously. This bad boss, when presented with those product ideas, had talked them down, and shown very little enthusiasm, and certainly given no recognition to my respondent for taking the initiative to come up with them. To then hear those very same ideas being discussed by this Director to his peers – within his hearing as if he didn't exist, was incredulous. Hearing your own material 'passed off' as the ideas of your boss is a morale killer.

Needless to say, my respondent found the impact of observing this conversation extremely demoralising. It made him wonder if he could ever gain any recognition for his work, or be acknowledged for his contribution. The fact that his boss wasn't even aware of his presence, or how it would make him feel, somehow made the situation worse. He began to formulate his plans to leave the business, and take his talents elsewhere – aiming to work for a boss who might appreciate his contribution.

What is your experience of stealing the work of others?

There are many situations where bad bosses take credit for the work done by others. Have you ever been tempted to claim the credit for something done by another? Have you actually done it? Did the individual witness it happening?

Are you the courageous leader who doesn't feel so exposed, so that they need to claim someone else's credit?

SUMMARY POINTS:

- Stealing the credit for the ideas and achievements of others is felt very keenly by followers – it hurts them!
- Claiming other's work as your own is a major credibility killer for followers.
- Bad bosses steal ideas because they lack courage and feel exposed to prove their worth. This is a doom loop which closes down followers.
- Good bosses have the courage to make brave changes, and recognise the contribution of the team members who contribute. This is a virtuous circle which generates more and better contributions.
- Have you ever felt the need to claim the work of others as your own?

YOUR ACTIONS:

Find out whether any of your team does this to their people. Determine that you will give your team and individuals public credit for their contributions. Build a virtuous circle of achievement and recognition.

CHAPTER 7 BAD BOSSES ARE GUILTY OF BEING POOR COMMUNICATORS

The inability to inspire others is a major fault in leaders

> "Great leaders are almost always great simplifiers, who can cut through argument, debate and doubt – to offer a solution everybody can understand."
>
> Colin Powell
>
> "Leadership is not just about giving energy, it's unleashing other people's energy."
>
> Paul Polman
>
> "Leadership is the capacity to translate vision into reality."
>
> Warren Bennis
>
> "The very essence of leadership is that you have to have a vision."
>
> Theodore Hesburgh

Number 7 in the top 10 Pitfalls of bad bosses

We are moving up the scale of traits of bad bosses. At number 7 is the inability to communicate and inspire your people. I heard this from numerous respondents.

Perhaps the most public example of this communication failing in recent times has been Prime Minister Theresa May. Her wooden speechmaking and lack of a compelling vision has inspired no one. It has been one of the profound reasons for her downfall, in my own view.

I have always argued that good communication is the 'rocket fuel' of a high performance culture! Conversely, it stands to reason that poor communicators make poor leaders. If it holds true (and I believe it to be true), that "the more they know then the more they will care", then the less they know the more detached followers will be.

I had a lot of feedback from my survey respondents, about bosses who were extremely poor communicators. The effects on organisations were always hugely negative, and caused serious morale and performance issues. A lack of effective communication down the levels of the organisation creates mistrust and hinders performance. How can a workforce help with problems if they don't really know what is going on?

This sort of bad boss issue isn't about the leader behaving badly. It's more of a leader underperformance problem, causing followers to be frustrated and disappointed. It certainly left my survey respondents with an underwhelming feeling of "if only they could inspire the teams".

The book of Proverbs Chapter 29 v 18

I make no apology for using a biblical reference, which certainly holds true in all circumstances. That Biblical quote from Proverbs is that "where there is no vision, the people perish." The Biblical vision was about God, and in the business context it is the company vision.

People working in companies today do not flourish without an inspirational communicator at the head, who can set a vision for them and their future. Employees aspire to do worthwhile work. People want their jobs to count for something. This is not just about making a profit alone. Profit is an important consequence of work, but it cannot be a raison d'etre. The 'reason for being' should be something that followers can believe in.

So many leaders are just maintainers. They keep things ticking along. They are professional, organised, but deadly dull. Bad bosses cannot bring the business to life. They do not have the ability to talk a compelling story to their followers. They actually fail to be 'storytellers' at all. Why would anyone want to follow you if you are a dull and boring leader?

Simon Sinek's book 'Find your why'

Simon Sinek argues, in his book, that many leaders begin by thinking about what they want to do, and then go on to think about how to do it. What and how are clearly important, but they should not be the beginning of the process.

The problem with bad bosses here, is that they do not think about the motivations of their people in the process. The source of that motivation does not come from what and how. Simon Sinek argues that people will only really 'buy in' to a new product/service/idea, if they understand the 'why' behind it. I fully agree with his premise. If you don't communicate your purpose to your people with skill, and the use of storytelling to bring it to life – they will not be inspired, and they will certainly not give you their discretionary effort.

Bad bosses simply do not get this concept at all. They think it is all about just doing the job. They fail to inspire their followers, and they don't see the importance of purpose in people's lives. The consequence is simple – people below them underperform. My survey respondents felt huge resentment about leaders they had worked for, who couldn't provide the required level of inspiring communication. People are always 'hungry' for knowledge, and they desperately want to be inspired. There is an energy to the process. Bad bosses just don't have it, and can't or won't do it.

John F Kennedy and the visit to NASA

The story I always use to illustrate this point, is the famous one concerning John F Kennedy visiting NASA. He is reputed to have asked a man sweeping a corridor what he was doing. He replied "we're here to put a man on the moon."

That is a classic illustration of a person in a fairly mundane job, who had been enthused by the vision of the team. I suppose, in the language of the motivational theorist Maslow, he was only a cleaner, but he was exhibiting traits of being self-actualised in his work.

Inspiration matters, and bad bosses don't seem to understand that simple perspective.

Ella's Kitchen – a brand that seems to understand purpose

Ella's Kitchen was established by a mother, whose baby had some allergy problems. She devised products which were suitable for her own baby, and then took them to a wider audience. Ella's Kitchen has subsequently become a well-established brand of organic baby food products. Ella's Kitchen is run by leaders who understand the importance of mission and purpose, and communicate that to their people in a relevant and individual way.

Everyone wants to be proud of the organisation they work for, and Ella's Kitchen bosses know that it's important to bring the mission and purpose to life for their people. They believe it is the foundation for everything that they do as an organisation.

That's a business which is not about to fall into the poor communication pitfall which so commonly occurs in businesses run by bosses who 'just don't get it'.

<u>'Bad Bosses' say things which come back to bite them later</u>

Some of my respondents talked about the communication errors made by CEOs they had worked for. One particular 'bugbear' was about those leaders who over-promised and under delivered. Those type of leaders were generally derided, because they agreed and set ludicrous/patently unachievable targets. There were a whole plethora of such examples given to me, where such leaders had just said and done the wrong thing.

In the view of the subordinates, this was a lack of maturity in communication. Those bad bosses who communicate poorly, clearly do not give anywhere near enough thought to what they are going to say, or how best to say it. If you intend to set a ludicrous target, at the bare minimum, you need to give context as to why, and give people the latitude to shoot for it, and give them a parachute if they fail. Storytelling and context are vital in all circumstances, rather than bare facts.

<u>'Bad Bosses' fail to flex their style of communication</u>

Really effective communicators can speak in Board rooms; to clever City investors; to cynical Press hacks; to middle managers and to their employees on the shop floor. All of those audiences need a subtly different style and approach, and the smart communicator knows exactly how to vary their approach.

The ability to tailor language and approach to your audience, is a requirement of the effective leader. 'Bad bosses' simply fail to adapt their communication style to the context, and thus fail to gain 'buy-in' to what they are saying.

Many of the respondents I interviewed, talked about CEOs they had worked for using jargon and being misunderstood by the workers on the shop floor. Ineffective jargon is incomprehensible in that sort of context, and serves to 'turn off' the workforce.

Some communication errors are about bad planning

One CEO told me a salutary story about himself, during his own early career. It takes courage to talk about your own mistakes, and I respected him for it. Most of my feedback had been from individuals talking about others!

In this case, during a big organisational change of reporting lines and structures, he had discussed everything with each of his team leaders, before making a more general announcement to the organisation as a whole. He felt sure that the whole communication process had gone well, until at the last moment, he realised that he had forgotten to brief one of his team leaders based elsewhere in the company.

This leader had to sit down with that individual, who had heard about the reorganisation in a general briefing, and apologise profusely for his error.

Years later, both of the people in this story were working for different organisations, and happened to bump into each other whilst travelling on business. They were able to recollect and laugh about that particular 'cock up' on the communication front, and look back fondly. That boss learnt 'the hard way' that he should prepare all his communication meticulously, and apologise swiftly and personally if he messed up in any way. A useful lesson for all leaders!

SUMMARY POINTS:

- Bad Bosses fail to communicate and inspire – the consequence being under-performance by their subordinates.
- Without a vision – the people working for you cannot flourish and outperform.
- Your people need to understand 'why' they are doing what they are doing – it's massively energising.
- People want and need to believe that what they do is 'worthwhile work'.
- Don't be rash in communicating things which come back to bite you.
- Flex your own style to speak differently to different types of audience – the message is much more likely to hit home if you are able to do this.
- Plan communication meticulously and apologise swiftly and personally if you 'screw it up'.

YOUR ACTIONS:

- Ask your people whether they understand the 'why' of your business. You may be surprised by the answers.

- Challenge your managers to become 'storytellers'. That capability to inspire makes a huge difference to morale and performance.

- Spend a lot more time planning how to get internal communications right and make them inspirational by intent.

CHAPTER 8 'BAD BOSSES' FAIL TO LIVE THE COMPANY VALUES PERSONALLY

Followers notice hypocrisy in leaders very quickly

> "Change will not come if we wait for some other person, or if we wait for some other time. We are the ones we've been waiting for. We are the change that we seek."
>
> Barack Obama
>
> "If ethics are poor at the top, that behaviour is copied down through the organisation."
>
> Robert Noyce

Number 6 in the top 10 pitfalls is an ethics issue

I have always told leaders, that the people working in organisations closely observe their leaders in everything they do and say. They look at what you wear; they listen to what you say; they clock the hours you keep; they note your level of commitment to the business. They know the car you drive; where you live; where you go on holiday. In short, they scrutinise everything about you as a leader. The scary thing for leaders, is that all this happens imperceptibly and casually. As a leader, many are totally unaware or conscious of this level of scrutiny – but it is happening nevertheless.

If your behaviour as a leader fits what you are saying more publicly, and also fits with the values of the business, then all will be well.

However, if you have an ethics failure, then you will be in trouble as a leader. Many of my respondents were particularly irritated by bad bosses, who felt they were able to ignore the company values – because they were 'above that sort of thing'. This type of behaviour is seen by followers as "do what I say, not what I do".

Subordinates become really angry when the company values they are being required to live by, are undermined by the behaviour of a senior leader. 'Bad Bosses' seem to think that they are able to go around the rules with impunity, 'because they are in charge' or "it's my company so I will do what I like". This is not so. People will most certainly notice, and will mark the leader down for their behaviour. The leader will lose integrity and trust, which are hugely difficult to build, but all too easy to lose. It is a huge cultural 'no-no' to ignore the values of the business, and will devalue what the business stands for. That belief that you strive for employees to hold, will be discounted, and some people will look to leave the business in these sort of regimes.

Make no mistake, senior leaders do have an obligation to live by what they say. Not to do so will downgrade the belief and performance of subordinates observing such behaviours.

'Bad Bosses' are seen as inauthentic

Those leaders who ignore company values undermine their personal authenticity. Pretending to be someone you are not in reality will be quickly spotted by those working around you.

Your people will discuss such behavioural breaches when you aren't around.

A survey of workforces in the UK by Warwick Business School recently, revealed that almost two thirds of workers surveyed had experienced serious unethical behaviour at work. That is an astonishingly high figure. Interestingly, 71% of those surveyed said that they wouldn't report the wrongdoing they observed or experienced for fear of reprisal or losing their position. This means that leader behaviour which undermines the business performance tends not to be reported, but its consequences in terms of morale and productivity loss will be tangible.

I would suggest that 'Bad Boss' behaviour is widespread in the UK, but no one talks in public about the subject, because they want to keep their job, and fear 'rocking the boat'. It's difficult to speak truth to power.

I'm reminded of that oft misquoted phrase – "the only thing necessary for evil to triumph, is for good men to do nothing."

I wonder how many leaders out there believe that no one has noticed their behaviour, because nothing has been said about it publicly? They are deceiving themselves, by fundamentally misunderstanding human behaviour in organisations. They may not tell you openly, but your credibility will be massively undermined, and you will begin to wonder why people do not want to go the extra mile for you. The source of that unwillingness is your own credibility, or the lack of it.

An example of leader hypocricy

One of my survey respondents talked to me about a company he worked for, which had a set of company values speaking about honesty; integrity and upholding family values. The CEO of that company espoused those values, and indeed had been part of the top team writing them in the first place.

Sadly, this same CEO, who talked those company values in public, was carrying out a clandestine affair with the company HR Director, despite being a married man himself. The affair quickly leaked within the company, with the resulting loss of integrity for the CEO and HR.

The hypocrisy of this sort of behaviour quickly becomes apparent, and is soon the topic of gossip around the business. Productivity and loyalty can never be enhanced by this type of situation, rather, individuals will withdraw discretionary effort as a consequence of their loss of trust.

Leaders should not be making employees cynical as a result of their own behaviour. Unfortunately, it happens all too frequently, and we read about it almost daily in our newspapers. Company statements of values and behaviours shouldn't be a list of 'nice to haves', which are merely words in a framed notice board on the wall in the lobby. They need to be a guide to the way that all leaders live on a daily basis.

Trust in leaders in public life varies by profession

The IPSOS MORI 'Veracity Index' for 2017 makes for interesting reading:

(Veracity is habitual truthfulness/accuracy/sticking to facts)	
Nurses	94%
Doctors	91%
Teachers	87%
Professors	85%
Scientists	83%
Judges	81%
Weather Forecasters	76%
The Police	74%
TV Newsreaders	67%
Clergy/Priests	65%
Person in the street	64%
Civil Servants	59%
Lawyers	54%
Pollsters	50%

Charity CEOs	50%
Trade Union Officials	45%
Local Counsellors	41%
Bankers	38%
BUSINESS LEADERS	36%
Estate Agents	27%
Journalists	27%
Professional Footballers	26%
Governments Ministers	19%
Politicians generally	17%

The IPSOS MORI Poll about who you can trust in life, is disastrous for Politicians (no doubt not helped by the UK MPs Expenses scandal). But it is not good for business leaders either.

For me, the weather forecast, despite expensive technological equipment, is frequently erroneous, but weather forecasters have a pretty high rating of trust at 76%. Yet business leaders, who should be of high integrity in running multi £million businesses have a poor 36% trust rating. This is still nowhere near good enough.

If you examine historical data, business leaders have improved their trust ranking over the past 20 years by around 10% - so there is still hope!! However, the scores remain at a concerning level. There are a lot of 'Bad Bosses' out there, whose integrity is dragging down those perception scores.

I think that the IPSOS MORI veracity index makes pretty depressing reading for a lot of the professions, and it is a real challenge to business leaders to 'step up to the plate' of honesty and integrity. Developing habitual truthfulness, and doing the right thing in all circumstances is the 'gold standard' of leader behaviour. It is also tested most at times of difficulty such as company redundancies or financial instability.

SUMMARY POINTS:

- Leaders are observed minutely at all times – never think otherwise – you are being carefully watched.
- Your people are watching to see if your words and actions fit with the values of the company.
- Ethical failures in leaders undermine trust in the company and affect performance.
- Serious unethical behaviour by business leaders is widespread, but often goes unreported because of fear in the workforce.
- Failing to live the company values leads to cynicism amongst employees and withdrawal of discretionary effort by them.
- Business leaders are currently in the bottom third of the veracity index amongst all professions. That just isn't good enough.

YOUR ACTIONS:

- Do you measure leader behaviour in living company values currently?
- If not, make this part of your anonymous employee engagement survey.

CHAPTER 9 'BAD BOSSES' ARE PRONE TO EXCESSIVE EGO AND HUBRIS

Arrogance breeds the view "it's all about me"

> "Level 5 leadership, shown by the most powerfully transformative executives, is a paradoxical mix of personal humility and professional will."
>
> Jim Collins
>
> "A great leader never sets himself above his followers, except in carrying responsibilities."
>
> Jules Ormont
>
> "Power corrupts and absolute power corrupts absolutely."
>
> Sir John Dalberg-Acton

Number 5 in the Pitfalls which most irritate followers

We are now entering the Top 5 leader behaviours which 'Bad Bosses' exhibit, and totally irritate their followers.

I've worked with many executives over the 45 years in business. Many of them truly believed "it's all about me". Their arrogance meant that they never fully leveraged the full potential of their teams. Those type of leaders almost never say "thank you" to subordinates, and tend to be 'status junkies' who are very aware of their position in the hierarchy. They are fixated on possessions, and the trappings of job status, they sit in big offices and hire 'Rottweiler' P.A.s to sit outside those big offices. You all know the type. I'm sure you will have worked for one of those at some time or other.

I remember, very fondly, one colleague I worked alongside, who had responsibility for the company car scheme, along with his responsibilities. He had a wicked sense of humour, and a levity about senior leader behaviours! He used to tell me that he could immediately tell whether a newly hired executive would succeed or fail in the business – by how much trouble they gave him over choosing and ordering their company car from the list. Those who were obsessed by status would want to have something not on the list at their level; they would want some sort of special alloy wheels; or in some way stretch the rules about some 'gizmo' they were wanting but weren't entitled to under the rules.

These signs of over emphasis on ego/status and pride were contra signals about their willingness to fit into the company culture. Their motivation wasn't to fit in and get on with the job – but was totally absorbed with "me, me, me". Invariably, my colleague's prediction about these individuals and their company car would be an illustration of their failure to truly join the culture, and act as a predictor of their subsequent departure from the business in question.

Personal ego and hubris usually have a poor outcome. 'Bad Bosses' have it, and followers loathe it.

Hubristic leadership is a 'turn off' for followers

A large number of my respondents highlighted 'hubris' as an irritant for them as followers. Hubris is that belief by the leader that they have some 'fairy dust' to solve problems, and that only they can resolve issues. Followers of this type of leader have to 'dance to your tune alone', and this type of behaviour is definitely something followers do not admire.

My respondents talked to me about leaders who they thought exhibited so much egotistical behaviour that they were seen to be 'smoking their own dope'. Leaders need to learn that it is not healthy to believe "it's all about me", and begin to leave their ego behind in order to get the best out of followers.

Henry Mintzberg talked about getting executives off their 'lofty perches'. Mintzberg felt that people who called themselves 'leaders' was at least half the problem. He believed that no authentic leader called themselves that. Mintzberg felt it was for followers to decide the title you hold. In other words, do your subordinates feel that you are worthy of the title of leader?

The now infamous Neil Woodford spent years as a great stock investment picker, until his hubris went to his head. That hubris became his downfall, and his empire has come tumbling down as a consequence. 'Bad Bosses' need to learn the lesson of humility rather than letting their ego take over.

The very success that made you can cause you to fail

Hubris is effectively over-confidence; over ambition and over-weaning pride in your own personal achievements, according to Eugene Sadler -Smith of Surrey Business School. These traits are mostly fuelled by prior success, and cause those successful individuals to have a contempt for the advice of others.

Sadler-Smith, quite rightly in my view, states that this type of attitude is a dangerous cocktail, which tends to lead executives to believe that things will go right, and to underestimate what can go wrong. Much of the last major global financial crisis caught such hubristic bankers off guard.

It is Sadler-Smith's view that strong leaders need to be tempered in hubristic/egotistical traits by trusted advisers or Non-Executives, who are able to read the signals where leaders are over-reaching themselves or their businesses.

It is very easy for leaders to begin to deceive themselves, particularly if they have had a fair measure of business success.

Self-Deception is the source of all hubris

Some executives have an amazing filtration process, which causes them to see everything in their world through one single lens – their own ego. Leaders who are unable to view the world from the point of view of others, have a serious problem. This can put such leaders offside with employees, customers and stakeholders.

All bosses need to realise that leadership is seductive. When you are in a leadership role, it is very easy to slip into the idea that you are better/smarter/special in some way than those around you. There are always individuals working in organisations who will help the leader to perpetuate those feelings. They are 'playing' to your ego, because they are managing their own career through you as their leader. They harness themselves to the momentum of the leader and say what the leader wants to hear. Such followers become "yes" people, and will agree with everything the leader says and does. Such follower behaviour serves to feed the leader's ego, bur adds no real value.

Leaders need to be aware that, if they are not very careful, they will be surrounded by 'group think'. A team of people who say yes to all that they suggest, and this can be utterly disastrous in times of crisis or major change. Hubristic leaders tend to be surrounded by 'groupies', and they do not see how harmful it has become.

Real leaders seek out and hire people who are better than themselves, and will challenge their thinking where necessary. That is the source of real strength. It is much harder to manage, but much more effective. It's the 'grit' of the forming pearl in the oyster. Strong leaders respect challenge, when it comes, and act accordingly.

The trouble is, that those big jobs; with big job titles; coupled with big workspaces and giant desks; those huge salary packages and that behavioural latitude to make big decisions – are all extremely beguiling. Leaders are rarely challenged, and feelings of superiority in the executive can grow very easily. Leadership brings positional power, and power can corrupt. Absolute power does corrupt absolutely! Power inflates the ego of the unwitting leader, and that hubris will land them in subsequent deep trouble. Hubris is a real leadership 'killer'.

Followers deride leaders who have no self-awareness

Ego and hubris are clearly huge 'no-no's' for the subordinates who are followers. Yes there will be sycophantic people gathered around such leaders, but smarter people won't believe the hubristic behaviour at all. Such a leader will never carry the goodwill of the whole organisation.

Those type of 'Bad Bosses' who are not self-aware, will not look for their blind spots and weaknesses. They perpetuate the myth that only one opinion really counts, and that is their own.

This is clearly a tough issue to tackle. It is common, because it is number 5 in the top 10 irritants for followers. Yet positional power is tough to challenge. Where the ego of the leader is especially strong, such 'Bad Bosses' tend to put down/destroy the reputation of those individuals with the temerity to give them any honest feedback. They will much prefer the sycophantic version of feedback that they are hearing from their 'groupies'. It takes a brave person to give honest feedback in such circumstances!

Consequently, honest feedback rarely comes from below the offending leader. It has to come from an external adviser or other more senior voices. It is, however, vital to deal with hubris and ego in the leader. Without this being tackled successfully, the leader will never perform to their potential, and nor will the organisation.

SUMMARY POINTS:

- Signs of leaders where "it's all about me", are over emphasis on the 'trappings' of executive status.
- Hubristic leadership is a huge turn off for sub-ordinates, and will lead to underperformance of teams.
- You should never call yourself a leader – that accolade must be designated by your followers.
- Hubris is an organisational danger signal that can have serious implications.
- Self-deception can be reinforced by a core of sycophantic followers, and 'group think'.
- Success is beguiling, and ego can build out of proportion very quickly and easily.
- External/Senior feedback is the only remedy for hubris and ego which is out of control.

YOUR ACTIONS:

- Measure the views of subordinates for hubris, which can be reported to you anonymously. If you are guilty of an inflated ego – take action to change style.

- Make sure senior leaders are tempered by the advice of external mentors or Non-Executives.

CHAPTER 10 'BAD BOSSES' JUST DON'T LISTEN

Failing to take feedback is dangerous for leaders

> "No one is a leader if there are no followers."
>
> Malcolm Forbes
>
> "It's a terrible thing to look over your shoulder when you are trying to lead – and find no one there."
>
> Theodore Roosevelt
>
> "A modern business leader is all about having your finger on the pulse, constantly learning, so that you know what you're talking about."
>
> Richard Branson

Not Listening – No 4 in the lexicon of 'Bad Boss' behaviours

I often talk about listening to others being the highest form of respect that we can show to others. We all like the courtesy of being asked for our opinion.

We've already established that ego and hubris make for poor listening leaders, because they lead people to believe subordinate views don't count for much. The listening aspect was drawn out by my respondents as a separate topic – such was its importance to them. Listening skills, or the total absence of them, came in for special mention as a particular irritant to followers.

Failing to listen to your people is a really bad signal for leaders to send. It quickly establishes that you don't value their opinion, and therefore you don't really value them. They realise you believe, as a leader, that only your own views count, and they will then leave you to produce all the answers and solutions. None of us individually is smarter than all of us, and so the non-listening leader will fail to answer all the issues that arise, in the most optimal way. Failing to take feedback causes opportunities to be lost; errors to be made/perpetuated; performance and morale to suffer. It's a 'doom loop' for leaders not to listen.

One respondent told me the story of a new MD, who failed to listen to their sales and marketing teams, regarding a new product. Because feedback was not taken, the product failed, and cost the business £250,000. The MD was fired because of the failure, just 12 months after his appointment. A pretty salutary example of a Bad Boss failing to listen with disastrous consequences for the business and for him personally.

<u>The mantra has to be 'Talk less – Listen more'</u>

Failing to listen to our people/and customers is a howling oversight. Their input to any situation can be invaluable.

My survey respondents talked at length about working for leaders who were constantly in 'transmit mode', rather than recognising the power of being in 'receive mode'. This, they said, was especially true in times of major change. They told me that leaders always tend to 'take over' any room they entered. It was their natural 'modus operandi' to fill the silence. Such leaders fail to realise the power of silence and subsequent listening.

It is very tempting for leaders to think that they already have access to all the information that they need to make any decision. However, forgetting to talk to the very people who make up our organisations – the hands/eyes and ears that produce our products and deliver our services day in and day out – is a huge omission. Leaders often believe that they know best, or in some cases may just be fearful of the feedback they may hear.

What these 'Bad Bosses' need to realise, is that spending some time listening on a regular basis, can produce dramatic and valuable insight into issues/problems and solutions. Problems can be picked up and remedied early, before they get to customers. New ideas can be elicited that the management team did not think about, because no one previously bothered to ask. Employees will also be energised by the very fact that leaders are prepared to listen to their opinion.

Talking with customers produces similarly healthy results. It is one thing to read customer survey data – but much more cathartic to hear it directly face to face. Nothing beats hearing things direct from the customer's mouth.

Leaders in all walks of life become remote all to easily

'Bad Bosses' are not just seen in business – this trait occurs in all walks of life. Politicians such as Margaret Thatcher; Tony Blair and Theresa May all became detached from real electors and their views about real issues. Messages get filtered and 'spun' by middle men, and politicians are quickly staring through a fog of misinformation.

Wherever people work with others, there is a need to show empathy for colleagues. We all need to listen to where others are forming views and opinions and why. Listening is not a sign of leadership weakness – but a show of great wisdom and strength.

Institute of Leadership and Management research

75% of employees in a 2017 ILM Survey, said that they wanted more freedom in their workplace. 66% of those surveyed responded that they struggled to fit into their place of employment.

Employees crave to be allowed to be more flexible, more innovative and more creative. Yet even in the 21st Century, work feels rigid and authoritarian to employees.

When asked what they would most like to see their bosses do, they said "leaders should get back to the shop floor more often, in order to elicit the views of their people." In effect, the survey was saying that employees want to be listened to by their leaders.

Non-listening by leaders is a major factor in employee labour turnover, yet 'Bad Bosses' probably never realise that fact to be true in their own businesses.

The listening standard set by Richard Branson

We would all recognise that Richard Branson is a larger than life entrepreneur. His whole business career has been extremely unconventional. He is great at P.R., and deploys zany and 'off the wall' tactics to his businesses.

One thing that Richard Branson is famous for, is this skill of listening to his people. His quote at the opening of this chapter – "being a modern business leader is all about having your finger on the pulse, and constantly learning, so that you know what you're talking about" – illustrates just how much he believes in the power of listening to other people.

Richard says that he is constantly connected and engaged with what his people are thinking. He also keeps copious notes of the things he is being told. He has his 'ear to the ground', in all corners of the globe, and constantly checks in with his Virgin teams. He makes full use of social media to assist him in knowing what his people and customers are saying. He takes the business of listening very seriously indeed. He values the process highly.

I've never actually worked with Richard, but what he says about the power of listening for leaders, is absolutely 'spot on' in my view.

Why don't all leaders 'listen to the river' on a regular basis?

If listening makes such eminent business sense, and top class world business leaders do it systematically, then why is this number 4 in the list of 'Bad Boss' behaviour irritants?

Is it that leaders get so busy that they don't find the time/or make the time to do it?

Is it that leaders simply don't value the thoughts and ideas of their employees and customers?

Is it that leaders truly believe they know everything that they are likely to hear already, and therefore don't want to waste precious management time?

Is it because leaders are fearful of conducting such a listening exercise because the might open a 'Pandora's box' of problems? Do leaders think their fear is a sign of weakness, and they shun listening as a consequence?

If you are a leader who doesn't systematically listen to employee and customer voice – then only you can answer the reasoning for yourself!!

In the real world, CEOs and Boards can never have all the answers. Belief in such a myth can never make it true. The world is so complex, ambiguous and fast changing, that leaders need all the help and input they can get. Organisations are moving at speed, and CEOs need a mechanic for seeking the views of a much broader group of people, with a wide variety of skills, than just their Board colleagues. Effective leaders have always encouraged their organisations to collaborate, and draw in input from varied sources. Listening is a key component of leader and business success.

SUMMARY POINTS:

- Failing to listen to your people is a bad cultural signal – it says you don't value what your people think.
- Talk less as a leader – listen more.
- Listening can provide early 'radar' on issues/solve intractable problems/be a rich source of great ideas.
- Listening to customers and employees is vital in knowing what is going on – it is invaluable – be smart.
- It's all too easy to become remote and rely merely on data analysis interpreted by 'advisers'.
- Employee frustration levels are high – often because no one listens to their innovative ideas, nor their suggestions – and they have no freedom to act.
- Why don't leaders 'listen to the river' of valuable opinion when it clearly works for top leaders?

YOUR ACTIONS:

- Determine to set up a mechanic to listen to your people and your customers on a regular basis.

- Ask yourself – what stops me from listening?

CHAPTER 11 FAILING TO MANAGE THE PERFORMANCE OF YOUR PEOPLE

A key expectation of followers – is that leaders manage the performance issues of the organisation

> "The situational leader changes his/her style, depending upon the person they are working with, and on the situation itself."
>
> Ken Blanchard
>
> "Capable performing people are the scarcest resource in any organisation."
>
> Peter Drucker
>
> "In an information society, people are any organisation's competitive edge."
>
> John Naisbitt

'Bad Boss' behaviour Number 3 – failing at the task of Performance Management

This is the 3rd most irritating behaviours to the followers in my survey. We are now getting to the really major things which annoy subordinates and 'switch them off' to leaders.

I have already written a book on the topic of 'Performance Management for the 21st Century'. I wrote the book, because I recognise that this is a subject which many leaders find difficult to do well. Many CEOs have told me, over the years that they struggle with this topic. So I was not at all surprised that this issue came up in the context of the behaviour of 'Bad Bosses'.

Failing to manage performance has widespread ramifications

Leaders tend to think that only they and their top team know all the facts about who is performing and who is not. This is a total fabrication!

In reality, everyone in the organisation knows who the good, the average and the poor performers are. They can see it around them as they work together. Their expectation of leaders in this area are massive. They expect leaders to deal with those people who do not 'pull their weight'.

When a leader effectively does little or nothing about poor performers, they downgrade the performance of everyone in their workforce. People begin to say "why should I care what happens here? Look at X, they don't pull their weight". These sort of comments don't get made to the leaders, but they will be thinking this to themselves, and it will be the subject of 'scuttlebut' in the workplace. The effect on overall performance will be hugely negative over time.

Poor Accountability leads to poor performance

Many of my respondents talked about bosses who were just incapable of holding people to account for their delivery of work. They could not conduct a challenging conversation with an individual when required.

They talked about working for bosses who accepted mediocrity, because they didn't want the hassle and conflict of managing performance. This is a deeply ingrained 'Bad Boss' behaviour trait, and is all about avoidance of leadership responsibility.

A common response in my survey, was that leaders all too often became too friendly or over familiar with employees, and couldn't then bring themselves to manage problem performance or behaviours. It is a fine line to walk with your people, to be approachable and friendly, without compromising your ability to be objective, and give the hard feedback also.

British bosses are often averse to conflict by their very nature. Not 'rocking the boat', and avoiding problem people becomes their behavioural default position. It's a real 'Bad Boss' cop out, but it happens frequently according to my survey. Make no mistake, followers hate this sort of avoidist behaviour in their leaders.

Using the 'willing horse' to pull the load

'Bad Bosses' keep on giving remits and more work to the people they know will deliver. They don't want to approach the 'awkward squad' who will have a thousand reasons as to why it can't be done in the timeframe. They know those people will not deliver on time and within cost, so they go to someone who will. It's always easier to give a task to the individuals who are willing and able. That's where the phrase 'give a task to a busy person and they will get it done', comes from.

It is obvious that the 'willing horses' will eventually become exhausted and very dissolutioned with the leader. The facts they see are that awkward lazy people get an easy ride, and the diligent capable people are overworked. Motivation is eroded, and performance will decline in these circumstances.

Ignoring Bad Hires – 'Bad Bosses' let things run too long

A number of my respondents wanted to mention that bad hires had been made by leaders into their companies, when it was quickly obvious they were not a good fit, or were much less capable than first thought.

One CEO commented to me that he didn't like dealing with those who failed to perform after being hired, and he actually owned the business! Even as owner, where it literally was his money, he still found it really difficult to manage underperformance!

It would seem that 'Bad Bosses' who recruit the wrong people, fail to listen to feedback a deal with the issue. The longer this situation goes on, the more corrosive it becomes to morale and performance of the organisation. It is massively visible to people at all levels in the business, and reduces performance quickly. Leadership are effectively sending messages that there is no real accountability if you underperform – exactly the opposite of what you should be doing as a leader.

Employees will begin to wonder who is ever going to tackle the problem, and this will become the constant subject of the 'grapevine' of organisational gossip.

<u>'Bad Bosses' have a tendency to 'go soft'</u>

One CEO told me about a 'Bad Boss' he had worked for, who very occasionally gave some much needed feedback concerning poor performance. However, when the individual receiving the feedback became upset, he totally softened the message with platitudes, to make the person feel better! This CEO obviously felt the need to be 'kind' rather than objective and fair.

The issue for 'softening' every piece of feedback, is that accountability doesn't happen. The 'Bad Boss' thinks they are being human, but in fact, they are reducing the discretionary effort of all the rest of their employees, who see the offender being 'let off the hook' yet again.

Employees will give you discretionary effort, if they believe in the mission and purpose of the enterprise, and also if they respect the leaders they are working for. That discretionary effort will not be given if the leader is not visibly undertaking the management of people's performance.

Leaders who cannot fix poor performers send a terrible message to the rest of the organisation. It will also be no secret. The organisation watches leader behaviour, and that omission will be spotted very quickly indeed.

Why would people lead in a way that reduces performance?

Many leaders have said to me that this reluctance to manage conflict is born of fear. Fear that they will get the whole 'feedback thing' wrong. Fear that they will end up being taken to an Employment Tribunal, and cost the company a lot of money. Fear that the conflict conversation will be challenged and they will not have sufficient evidence to countermand the response. Fear that they will be subject to angry or tearful responses. The fears go on and on.

Leaders also realise that managing underperformance is extremely time consuming. There is a great deal of preparation required, and then the actual conversations and time for improvement take lots of diary space. This time hungry aspect, coupled with the fact that the leader sees the whole process as very negative for themselves, means they can always find something else which is more urgent and important, to deal with.

The fact that 'Bad Bosses' don't realise the impact of their conflict avoidance behaviour, is extremely serious. If such leaders realised how much collective employee goodwill and effort was being lost, they would pay far more attention to this topic which irritates followers so much.

SUMMARY POINTS:

- Bad performance management is an affliction of many leaders.
- All employees watch very carefully whether their leaders tackle underperformance – it is highly visible and very toxic when 'left to run'.
- Poor accountability causes even good people to work less hard.
- 'Bad Bosses' give extra work to busy willing employees, and go around the problem people.
- 'Bad Bosses', when hiring someone who doesn't fit, wait far too long in tackling the problem.
- 'Bad Bosses' feel the need to 'soften the blow' when giving feedback to underperformers.
- Kindness should not be construed as fairness.
- 'Bad Bosses' don't realise that ignoring performance management reduces the discretionary effort across the business.

YOUR ACTIONS:

- Make performance management feedback something that happens every month in your organisation.
- Read 'Performance Management for the 21st Century – the seismic shift to regular performance coaching', also by David Smith, available to order on Amazon, as a physical or ebook.

CHAPTER 12 BAD BOSSES ARE BULLIES

Bullying can take many forms – essentially it is an abuse of power in the Employer-Employee relationship

> "Leadership is linked to the exercise of power, so that a vision can be realised through the mobilisation of resources. Effective leaders need to have developed a high level of people skills. Leadership requires the development of key aspects of character, of balancing ambition with conscience, so that the individual can harness drive with the desire to be held fully responsible for their words and deeds."
>
> Andrew Kakabadse
>
> "Leadership appears to be the art of getting others to want to do something you are convinced should be done."
>
> Vance Packard

Bad behaviour permeates the hierarchy – it is No2 in the list of most hated behaviours

In the same way that a good example inspires others to act in a similar way, a 'Bad Boss' who bullies, will cause others in the hierarchy to follow that lead.

I've seen the behaviour of bullying bosses during my own career (and I'm sure that you the reader will have too!!). Their actions were by diktat, and they were the living embodiment of the 'command and control' style of leadership. Their power came from their position in the hierarchy, and their style was designed to create fear. Bullying bosses always seemed to derive pleasure from that exercise of power over others. Ultimately, they tended to gather some 'mini-me's' around them, who were also willing to emulate and replicate the bullying tactics of their leader.

Needless to say, followers hate this sort of working environment, and there are serious consequences.

Inappropriate behaviour drives the best people away

In my own experience, I observed a very senior married executive trying to coax females in the workplace into a relationship with him, using positional power. The people he approached were also married, and both subsequently left that business, due to his unwarranted attention. That executive was a serial philanderer, who drove talent out of every organisation he worked in.

There are constant examples in the press almost weekly of this type of bullying behaviour. I wonder how many talented people left the Ted Baker organisation over the years, due to the unusual behaviour of Ray Kelvin?

It is always the most talented people who leave quickly in a toxic culture. They are on speed dial to the headhunters, and are extremely marketable. A bullying culture will always shed good people fastest.

The News media are constantly reporting bullying allegations against executives

Whether it is the Speaker of the UK House of Commons, John Bercow, or the retailer Philip Green, bullying accusations are constantly flying around in the News media.

I was amazed to read about a domestic abuse charity CEO, Sandra Horley, being accused in the Times of creating an abusive and bullying environment for her people.

News media in 2019 reported bullying; sexual harassment and toxic work culture at Sellafield Nuclear plant.

Nike in Oregon ousted a handful of executives in 2018 due to their behavioural issues. Employees at Nike had been complaining about a corporate culture of bullying, and they said that it had been a 'bruising' place to work. It was also interesting to note that the executives who left Nike in 2018 because of bullying behaviour, were both men and women.

Even Judges in the UK have been reported as the main source of bullying in the legal profession. More than

50% of 1500 barristers questioned believed that the problem of bullying was 'alive and well' in their profession, and the source of that bullying was the judiciary!

Stories abound concerning bullying and sexual harassment

My respondents gave me a plethora of examples of bullying and sexual harassment in their workplaces.

Some CEOs 'wrote off' the careers of subordinates just 'on a hunch', and because they had the power to do so. Other such 'Bad Bosses' constantly delivered fire and brimstone speeches to entire management teams, whilst top performing people were part of the audience. Punishing the whole for the errors of the few is a cardinal sin for the leader – yet so many respondents quoted incidents of this.

One particular bullying tactic reported to me, was to always demand more, even when performance had been excellent. The bully is never ever pleased or satisfied. Some bullies were reported for making the lives of their subordinates so utterly miserable, that they would eventually leave the businesses. In many cases, respondents told me that the self-esteem of such victims was utterly destroyed.

One particular CEO seemed to feel it was appropriate, after a sales downturn, to give the whole conference gathering a severe roasting; sending them out for coffee, and suggesting that those who felt they weren't up to the job should leave their car keys outside and depart forthwith.

Other respondents told me that many 'Bad Bosses' used a deliberate 'divide and conquer' approach to leadership. Even after good overall sales figures, they believed in making speeches to management teams designed to 'bring everyone down a peg or two'. This sort of behaviour would always result in morale and sales decline afterwards. No wonder.

Another respondent told me of ritual humiliations carried out by his Sales Director. Those who had hit their sales figures were made to sit on one side of the table, whilst those poor unfortunates who had not hit plan would be seated on the other side of the table. This 'Bad Boss' then made available his 'words of wisdom' for the occasion "you lot (those who failed to hit plan) need to learn from that lot (those who had made plan). The CEO fired this Sales Director eventually, but not before a lot of collateral damage, and the loss of some very talented people from the business.

One 'Bad Boss' in a Midlands car factory was famous for threatening his 4 direct reports with dismissal every single week, and when particularly riled, he would throw objects such as staplers at individuals in his team.

All of these stories serve to illustrate that corporate bullies are alive and 'functioning' in the current era – despite all efforts to provide a better workplace. What are the types of bullies out there?

Ken Blanchard's 6 forms of bullying behaviour

Ken Blanchard identifies 6 ways in which 'Bad Bosses' can bully their subordinates:-

i. Condescending behaviour – patronising behaviour which dismisses the contributions of others. Bullies minimise the accomplishments of others in order to maximise their own.
ii. Wounding with sarcasm – sarcasm belittles others. It may be the lowest form of wit – but it hurts.
iii. Bosses being cliquish – excluding certain people from activities is a form of bullying. It says "you're not one of us".
iv. Bosses who know it all – playing the 'all-knowing' superior is a way of intimidating others to get your own way and ignore them.
v. Being passive aggressive – bullying can take the form of veiled threats – using jokes/stubborn responses and even procrastination.
vi. Gossip – 'Bad bosses' use gossip to make themselves powerful above others.

I'm sure there are many other forms of bullying than the ones Blanchard identifies. I've certainly seen many others in my time, and I'm sure you have also. It is certainly true, that in the modern world, no bullying behaviour can have a good outcome. You can frighten people for a while, but the best will begin looking for another job very quickly.

The use of fear to brook no debate

A 2018 survey of UK employees revealed that 50% experience fear at work. It seems that fear has become a 'legitimate tool', used by leaders without scruples. This sort of behaviour is a driver of mental health problems; stress in the workplace; and underperformance generally.

The corporate bully might not look like the playground bully at all. Executives can use the threat of humiliation; withdrawal of available overtime; blocking of promotion opportunities and a whole host of tactics to silence critics and contrary voices.

Executive bullies are not necessarily drawn from one personality type. The most pernicious corporate bully is able to come across as polished and sophisticated to some audiences. They tend to be smart, but essentially use their intelligence to wield 'my way or the highway' type tactics. They sometimes even ask for ideas at the same time they are 'playing games' with subordinates. These type of 'Bad Bosses' leave that employee voice unheard. They can take untenable financial risks without challenge, and often brilliant ideas from subordinates never see the light of day.

Corporate bullies have a strong tendency to 'shoot the messenger' who brings bad news. They can be seen frequently punishing those individuals who bring unwanted news or views. This sort of behaviour is especially harmful to top teams, where there is no real discussion of serious decisions for fear of reprisal and loss of office.

It is very disconcerting to realise that this archaic and unacceptable type of behaviour is so prevalent in the 21st Century. So common that it is the 2nd on my list of 'Bad Boss' behaviours which followers hate most.

A glaring example of humiliation and bullying

This story was given to me by one of my respondents, and I have changed the names to protect any recognition of the characters involved. The context is an Estate Agency, where executives met the top guy, (let's call him Trevor), for a management meeting every Monday. Trevor would set the executives a task every week, and would require them to report back at this meeting.

The task on this particular week, had been relatively simple – to write out 10 reasons why 'Joe Public' should use this Estate agency, and not the competition down the street. At the Monday morning meeting, Trevor turned to the first member of the management team, and said "right Karen, what 10 reasons did you write down?" Karen said, "I'm really sorry Trevor, I had a really busy week, and I didn't get around to this." Trevor looked thunderous and replied "Karen, do I look like an idiot?" Karen was flabbergasted, and obviously didn't know what to say in return. There was apparently an awkward silence, with most of the management team staring at the table top in order to avoid eye contact with Trevor. Trevor spoke again: "Karen......do I look like an idiot?" More awkward silence ensued. Trevor (now standing and shouting for emphasis) – "Karen, I said, do I look like an idiot?" eventually, Karen quietly replied "No you don't."

Trevor proceeded to rant about the importance of his Monday meetings, and abruptly ended the session and stormed out.

I don't think the reader will be surprised to hear that Karen resigned later that very morning. Four Estate agents followed her out of the organisation within a couple of months. Bullying bosses drive labour turnover. People leave 'Bad bosses' not companies.

"Punishments will continue until performance improves"

This old-fashioned style of 'Bad Bosses' bullying others is alive and well in the modern era. Despite the fact that we think we are now educated and know better. It is widely understood intellectually that bullying cannot succeed in the long term, and yet it is obviously being deployed by bad leaders on a wide front, and in a variety of forms.

There is too much media reporting of bad behaviour in businesses. I should not be able to randomly quote so many examples about household names such as Nike and Google. These firms are purported to be exemplar employers.

Despite the expose of Harvey Weinstein and Jimmy Saville – it has been possible for sexual harassment predators to hide in plain sight in a number of contexts.

This sort of behaviour needs to be measured in leadership surveys and rooted out of leader behaviour. It should not exist in a sophisticated 21st century workplace environment. It cannot remain the second most common hated behaviour amongst bad leaders. Where does your own business stand on this?

SUMMARY POINTS:

- Bullying begets bullying – bad examples encourage other leaders to behave in similar ways.
- Sexual harassment and bullying drive labour turnover amongst your best talent – especially female talent.
- News media are full of reports of bullying and harassment – it's a weekly occurrence.
- Many respondents surveyed gave 'toe curling' examples of shouting/screaming/humiliation and hurling objects – that the horror of what 'Bad Bosses' are doing became embarrassing.
- Half the employees surveyed in 2018 expressed feeling fear from the behaviour of their boss.
- Fear closes down feedback, leads to bad decision making, and demotivates teams.
- Bullying and harassment blunt performance – yet are still commonplace amongst bad leaders.

YOUR ACTIONS:

- Rigorously measure leader behaviour – and stamp out bullying and sexual harassment.
- Bosses need to understand that this sort of behaviour is unacceptable in the modern workplace. They should know that it will be discovered and punished.

CHAPTER 13 BAD BOSSES ARE INSENSITIVE: THEY JUST DON'T CARE ABOUT THEIR PEOPLE

Insensitive leaders use people just like machines

> "Being a leader is more than just wanting to lead. Leaders have to show empathy for others, and a keen ability to find the best in people.....not the worst.....by truly caring for others."
>
> Henry Gruland
>
> "Don't forget to do something for other people."
>
> Marc Beniott
>
> "Leadership is about making others better as a result of your presence, and making sure that impact lasts in your absence."
>
> Sheryl Sandberg
>
> "If you command wisely, you'll be obeyed cheerfully."
>
> Thomas Fuller

<u>Work is not – nor should it be – totally transactional</u>

I'm sure we've all come across leaders who say "What's wrong with them, they get paid well don't they?"

This belief that work is something you do just for a wage or a salary, is very early 1900's 'Taylorist' thinking. F.W. Taylor was wrong when he first propounded his theory about the behaviour of people in the workplace. It was wrong then, and it is more wrong today. The motivational theorists of the 1950s onwards, such as Maslow; Elton Mayo; Herzberg and MacGregor thoroughly and comprehensively trounced this incorrect view of the employment contract. Motivation is about many more things than just money.

There is a 'psychological contract' with the people we employ, which involves many more facets than merely cash reward for effort.

The mission and purpose of the enterprise, over and above simple profit, matters to the people employed there. People want an ethical reason for doing what they do every day in the workplace. The personal characteristics of the leader they work for, and how they treat their people also matters hugely. As I have frequently argued, people leave their bosses if they are not happy with their treatment by that boss. They don't leave an abstract thing like a company.

If a 'Bad Boss' shows you no real feelings; fails to celebrate your successes; and makes it clear that your presence in the workplace is purely transactional. You will quickly become dissatisfied; dissolutioned; and give less than your best in terms of effort and initiative. Ultimately, if you are able, you will look to find another job.

The Number 1 reason for demotivated followers

Even above the obvious horrors of workplace bullying and sexual harassment – the feelings of being ignored; undervalued and unappreciated loom largest in this litany of poor leader behaviour!!

My survey respondents told me so many stories about CEOs they had worked for who would say "I don't care, I don't even want to know – just get on with what I pay you to do." These sort of 'Bad Bosses' never supported their teams, especially when they made a mistake. There was no sense in which their boss gave them 'air cover' for the organisational criticism flying around when things were going wrong. The bad bosses would merely stand aside and let their subordinates get the blame. In fact, 'Bad Bosses' would tend to add to the humiliation of people, rather than seek to protect them from it.

One such 'Bad Boss' was described to me – he was sitting back in a Board meeting whilst a member of his team took criticism and blame whilst presenting to the Board. He did not step in to help his subordinate, but merely weighed in with the rest of the Board in humiliation and ridicule. Sadly, this type of behaviour amongst leaders is common, but totally unacceptable.

An MD I was told about, was famous for creating 'pain' for his teams deliberately. This occurred in a retail business, where a particular team was charged with creating a new format 'store of the future'. It was a huge pressure project, entailing a lot of late night effort, with a good team spirit. At the grand opening of this pilot store, which took place on time and within budget (with 300 customers queueing outside the doors before opening) – the MD in question turned up and found a single poster missing from a wall, and spent his time criticising the team for their lack of detail. "Retail is detail" was his mantra, but his input was poison. He managed to turn a triumph into a deflating and demoralising occasion. He left his team feeling angry and resentful.

This kind of insensitivity 'grates' in the telling. Your reaction when hearing it is "how could he be so stupid?" However, it must seem perfectly acceptable to those 'Bad Bosses' who perpetrate these sort of things. They seem to be the kind of 'Bad Bosses' who just 'don't get it' about people and their feelings. They have little or no appreciation about how badly their behaviour affects morale. I suppose in modern parlance, we would say that 'Bad Bosses' of this type have a low EQ (Emotional Quotient) as opposed to a low IQ.

Not caring is a massive 'switch off' for discretionary effort

Some 'Bad Bosses' seem to be disconnected from people, and have an ability to ignore them. I'm sure we've all walked around a business premises, with the type of leader who knows everyone, and greets them all personally as they walk by. Sharing a few anecdotes and in jokes with their people. They obviously know their people well, and are admired and liked by them. It is highly motivational to conduct this type of walk round, and is the sign of a connected and highly effective leader.

In my own retail days, I could not possibly have a personal knowledge of 175,000 people. However, I regularly walked shop floors with a member of the management team, being introduced to people and spending a little time hearing about their career history and circumstances. They were obviously pleased to have attention and a little piece of limelight with a Board executive, and doing this sort of thing was expected, and it mattered to them. Humans enjoy attention! It's not rocket science.

Conversely, those leaders who seem to live inside their own heads, have the ability to walk around the workplace and speak to no one, are viewed with contempt by their people. They are so much in their personal 'bubble', that they have the ability to 'blank' employees who say "hello" to them. They seem to have no idea just how bad this sort of behaviour looks, nor how much it will worry and demotivate their subordinates.

One respondent told me of such a 'Bad Boss'. She was a new Director to the company, attending a team awayday. She asked everyone to introduce themselves (good), but said that she wouldn't remember them because she was terrible with names (bad). There were only 17 people in the room, and they were her key contacts. She then proceeded to spend the remainder of the awayday with her phone on her knee, reading emails and ducking out to answer calls. Needless to say, no one in the room felt valued, and no one was impressed by their new boss.

In another situation, a new Chair joined a business. She changed the dates of all the set Board meetings for the forthcoming 12 months, because the dates didn't work with her schedule of tennis matches (not a good start). She also, subsequently, lied to the CEO about another Board member. When challenged, she defended with the phrase "I'm in charge because I'm in the Chair." My respondent lost all confidence in this Chairperson, and left the organisation as a direct consequence. It doesn't take a lot of insensitivity to unseat talent in a business, but this is the last thing a leader should be doing.

These type of 'Bad Bosses' are the sort who seem able to dismiss people by text, without discussion. They seem to have had their personal 'sensitivity chip' surgically removed, and have very low to no emotional intelligence. EQ is just as vital as IQ in a leader, and it is frequently more important in getting the best out of others.

Failing to realise how your people are going to feel

Executives are prone to the delusion of living in a privileged world. Their status, their cars, the perks of office take them away from harsh reality. They just don't see things from the point of view of their workers.

One respondent told me about a situation where the company was really struggling, and the workforce were worried about job security. The new CEO came in and felt he was justified in spending a large sum of money to refurbish his executive suite. He lost all respect of his leadership team, and the workforce was stunned by the waste.

Another respondent told me about his business partner (they were joint MDs at the time), who turned up to work in a brand new Range Rover, in the very week they had to freeze all wage increases and cut 10 jobs from the firm because of market conditions. Needless to say, they are no longer business partners. He felt unable to work with a fellow executive who was so insensitive to those working for him.

Even more incredibly, one of my respondents recounted a similar situation of insensitivity. He was working as a CEO in a firm engaged in a fairly serious restructure. They were about to issue redundancy notices to 50 people, in a business of 350 people, so this was a major downsizing, and fairly traumatic for all involved since these were the first redundancies in the history of the business. On the day the redundancy notices were to be issued, the chairman turned up outside the office in his brand new custom made £150,000 Bentley. The CEO spotted him, and ran downstairs immediately to tell the chairman "what on earth were you thinking? Get that thing out of here. How could you be so insensitive to how people will be feeling today?" Apparently, the chairman felt his new car would cheer people up! He sheepishly drove it out of sight. Obviously a chairman with a low EQ!

I was also told about a CEO taking the decision to freeze the wages of all junior employees, whilst at the same time 'signing off' pay increases for Directors, including himself. This sort of insensitivity is palpably ridiculous when you see it written down on paper. Yet, these sort of insensitive actions are taking place in workplaces on a daily basis. No wonder this is the number 1 reason which most irritates followers.

Belittling subordinates is easy – but damage is permanent

I often say to audiences when I speak, that recognition done well lasts for a lifetime. That is certainly true.

The same is true for 'Bad Bosses' who belittle or ridicule their subordinates. You may think this rarely happens, but my survey yielded many extremely unfortunate and painful examples of such behaviour by leaders. So many executives are prone to give belittling and cutting comments – lashing out with little or no thought for the implications.

One respondent told me about a 'cringeworthy' experience, where the MD criticised one team member cruelly, with real humiliation, in front of their peers. The individual concerned was so affronted, that they stormed out of the meeting never to return to the business. Other team members were so affected and destabilised by the incident, it caused quite a few people to feel that they no longer wanted to work in the business. They began looking around for other roles.

'Bad Bosses' seem to perpetrate 'car crash' situations. I was told about a situation at an Awards ceremony in a business, where a senior leader ripped up a 'Certificate of Achievement' destined for an individual, in front of his colleagues, because the boss was unhappy with something about his performance that week. The punishment certainly did not fit the 'crime' in that case, and the incident became legendary for all the wrong reasons.

In another incident, again at an Awards ceremony for the company, the CEO said to the whole gathered audience "those of you who have won an award tonight, are just the best of the losers". What a way to turn a motivational occasion into total dissolution. What was he thinking?

Uncaring and insensitive behaviour appears to be rife

Being in a position of power does not, and cannot, condone inhuman and impersonal behaviour towards others. People are not robots. They have feelings which affect their ability to perform. Employment is not just a financial transaction.

Leaders would do well to realise that uncaring; insensitive or humiliating behaviour is the primary characteristic of 'Bad Bosses' that followers hate the most above all others. If it rises above bullying and sexual harassment, then it must receive due attention, and be rooted out of organisations.

SUMMARY POINTS:

- Work is not just a transaction – people come to work for many more reasons than the money.
- Being insensitive to people is the No1 reason why followers are irritated with their leaders.
- Not caring about your people 'switches off' any discretionary effort – it forces them into merely transactional relationships when they wanted more.
- 'Bad Bosses' don't possess great EQ. They don't seem to realise the negative effects of insensitivity.
- Belittling followers is easy from a position of power, but the negative effects will be permanent.
- Insensitivity is worse than bullying and sexual harassment, in the eyes of followers. They want leaders to care about them.

YOUR ACTIONS:

- Is this insensitivity exhibited by any leaders in your organisation?
- Measure leader behaviour and emphasise that any such tendencies will kill discretionary effort. Leaders need to behave better than this inexcusable style.

CHAPTER 14 WHAT TYPES OF BOSSES ARE OUT THERE? HOW DO YOU SPOT THE GOOD ONES?

There are good bosses and bad bosses

> "We run like mad, and then we change direction."
>
> Bert Roberts
>
> "The person who trusts people will make fewer mistakes than the person who distrusts them."
>
> Conte DiCamillo Benso Cavour

The 7 Types of Boss – which type are you?

Bosses are not all equal, and nor are they equally effective. Commentators have suggested 7 broad types of boss:-

i. The Overbearing Parent: they act like you're part of the family, and generally expect more from you than they should. Anything you do is because of them and for them. Unless you really are a family member, this is not a good boss to find yourself working for.
ii. The Mentor: this type of boss is the ideal. Your success is their success. They are fair, and share their expertise with you readily. Your achievements are

credited to you, and not stolen by them. This is a boss to seek out if you don't have it, or to value if you do.

iii. The Wastrel: they behave outrageously, and think it's funny. They want to be looked after by you, and you will be expected to cover for their failings. This is a type of boss to avoid or to leave.
iv. The Pariah: they are abrasive; aggressive and universally disliked in the organisation. People avoid working in their team or area. If you find yourself put with a pariah, find ways to build alliances elsewhere, and find a way out fast.
v. The One way User: impersonal and insensitive. They use you, and others, purely as a resource for their own ends. They will steal your work, and take all the credit without a second thought. Get out from this sort, and move on as fast as you can.
vi. The Wimp: they are insecure and thin skinned. Vulnerable in every way, they will refuse to let you or any other team member shine, because of their insecurity. No one wants to work for them.
vii. The Know it all: they are never wrong. They shout orders, to be obeyed without question. All they require are arms and legs to do their bidding. Don't bring your brain to work. Avoid if you can.

It's rather depressing that there are 6 'Bad Boss' types and only one type to seek out (the Mentor). You can see these types of Boss causing the problems followers hated in my survey.

The critical question is, how do you spot the 'Bad Boss' before you end up working for one? That is not always evident at interview, or at first sight. It might be worth concocting some interview questions to tease out the style of any potential leader. The problem then is that 'Bad Bosses' will probably lie about their style.

Another question worth asking – what type/style of boss are you with your own subordinates? What would they say about you?

Forbes 10 signs of a terrible leader

Forbes have defined 10 tell-tale signs of a 'Bad Boss', which might be of use to executives on the move to pastures new! These are the key characteristics to be aware of:-

i. A lack of Empathy
Caring for others and showing compassion is not a leadership weakness. Great leaders know the importance of empathy – poor leaders do not. Look out for signals about empathy with you.

ii. Bosses who fear change
Change is always scary and unpredictable, but change will always be happening, like it or not. Great leaders see change through the lens of opportunity. Poor leaders panic, and are made anxious by the unfamiliar.

iii. Bosses who never practice humility
Showing weakness is a strength. 'Bad Bosses' never own up to errors. Mistakes are never theirs, they feign perfection. Good leaders don't take

themselves too seriously, and are always approachable.

iv. <u>'Bad Bosses' avoid confrontation</u>
Confronting difficult people and underperformance situations is tough. 'Bad Bosses' fear being exposed by their own lack of knowledge, and hope the problem will just go away. The good leader tackles issues early, 'nipping problems in the bud', before they grow bigger.

v. <u>'Bad Bosses' are poor communicators</u>
Weak leaders are made most evident by their inability to communicate well. 'Bad Bosses' are unable to get their points across with impact. Poor leaders don't inspire people with a clear vision, and they don't seem to utilise storytelling. They just don't hack it. You can spot this failing from a mile away!

vi. <u>'Bad Bosses' are indecisive</u>
Poor leaders are 'wishy washy' around decision-making. They delay, ask for more and more data, and avoid coming to a course of action. Teams always require a clear action plan from the leader.

vii. <u>With 'Bad bosses' – it's all about them</u>
This is another trait of 'Bad Bosses' which is easy to spot. They are concerned to look good at all times. They talk about themselves incessantly. At interview, it will all be about them and almost nothing about you. Self-centred bosses never recognise the outperformance of others in their team.

Since it is all about them, they will take team credits. Great bosses mentor and sponsor their people, and encourage the development of others.

viii. <u>Work-Life balance is 'out of wack'</u>
'Bad Bosses' are workaholics. They are first in and last out. No one knows about their home life, because they remain stoic and detached from other people. 'Bad Bosses' tend to be machines heading for 'burn out', and present a bad role model for subordinates. Good bosses show vulnerability, and are much more normal people. Workaholics will burn you out with them.

ix. <u>Bad Bosses break their promises</u>
Doubt and mistrust surround bosses who say one thing and do another. Your name, as a leader, is only as good as your word. If you pledge something, you must move heaven and earth to do what you said you would do. 'Bad Bosses' speak, and don't even remember what they said by the following day.

x. <u>'Bad Bosses' micro manage</u>
'Checkers' tend to demotivate, and it's easy to spot the micro manager. They spend much of their time 'nit-picking' on minutiae, and lose focus on the all-important bigger picture. If you find a leader doing your job for you, then why are they paying you? Great leaders give clear remits and leave you to get on. They spend their time on external trending and bringing new ideas to the business.

Further thoughts on 'Bad Bosses' and their effects

It is sad to reflect that many of these tell-tale signs, as defined by Forbes, are all too familiar in places of work. They also correlate fairly closely with the results from my own survey.

The effect on morale, motivation and ultimately productivity is profoundly negative. Moreover, bad behaviour by the CEO or MD gives unscrupulous followers in middle management the legitimacy to copy that very bad behaviour themselves.

All this leads to the ongoing thought, that it is hugely important to measure leadership behaviours in any organisation on a regular and systematic basis. The importance of Engagement surveys and 360 feedback for leaders, cannot be over emphasised. How can we really know whether any of this bad behaviour is lurking in the hierarchy of our own organisations, unless we measure employee feedback anonymously?

Why do we tend not to hear about 'Bad Boss' behaviour?

In a 2019 UK survey, workers revealed that their reluctance to raise behavioural issues with their manager, if they were the problem, was down to fear. A real fear exists in organisations, that negative feedback about poor leader behaviours would cause those leaders to remove people from their jobs. At the very least, even if they didn't actually lose their job, then life could be made very difficult for them.

35% of all workers responded in the survey, that they would not raise it as an issue with their line manager. If other survey statistics, previously discussed in this book, reveal fear amongst 50% of the respondents in the workplace, I'm surprised that anyone has the courage to put their 'head above the parapet', and give feedback up the line. Speaking truth to power is a tough task, and takes enormous courage.

My strong urging to those of you in positions of power reading this book, is to pursue the measurement of the behaviour of your leaders regularly. Anonymous 360 feedback can reveal hidden issues if carefully constructed. I have used it to great effect, and it is often surprising to those receiving the results, just what their teams really think about their behaviour as a leader.

Cathartic change in leaders can only come as a result of quality feedback and follow up. The issues have to be exposed in order to act upon them.

SUMMARY POINTS:

- What type of leader are you?
- Only the 'Mentoring' boss really nurtures talent, and gives individuals chance to deliver and grow.
- There are ways to spot ineffective leaders. Tell-tale signs about managing change; inspirational communication; facing conflict effectively; good decision-making; and humility. Such facets can be included in feedback surveys. If they are not evident in a leader, then there will be an issue to address.
- 'Bad Bosses' kill morale and productivity.
- It's vital to measure leader behaviours anonymously. You won't hear about poor behaviour in any other way.

YOUR ACTIONS:

- Do you have an effective feedback measurement tool for leader behaviour in your organisation?
- Do you use feedback regularly and take action on bad leader behaviour?

CHAPTER 15 CONCLUDING THOUGHTS ABOUT 'BAD BOSSES' VERSUS GOOD BOSSES

Is it Emotional Intelligence which is the differentiator?

> "If you look for the best in people, you get the best from them."
>
> Richard Branson
>
> "L Look and listen: using senses/feelings/soul.
>
> E Empowerment: raises the status of leader and follower.
>
> A Awareness: what is my purpose? Inspiring followers.
>
> D Doing: action/doing what you say/cheering success.
>
> E Emotional freedom/Empathy: cut fear and anxiety.
>
> R Responsibility: showing initiative – taking mature risks.
>
> S Synchronicity: the ability to make good outcomes."
>
> Deepak Chopra

<u>'Bad Bosses' may be clever – but don't have good people skills</u>

When Daniel Goleman wrote about Emotional Intelligence, in the mid 1990s, he 'opened a window' on the reasons why some leaders are good with people. CEOs like Indra Nooyi at Pepsico, and Howard Schultz at Starbucks had great success because of their ability to deal with the so-called 'softer skills'.

However, there are always contra examples. Steve Jobs was famously low on EQ, and probably subscribed to the 'treat 'em mean, keep 'em keen' school of leadership. He had great success more by force than by encouragement.

The argument about leadership is not just about EQ versus IQ, and these are not the only determinants of success in a leader. Though, I would argue that Emotional Intelligence does certainly have a part to play in being a leader.

One thing I have observed in my own career, which spans over 40 years, is that people leave bosses rather than companies. I have said this before, and it is worth repeating again. The ability to understand and connect with people matters in retention of talent, and EQ plays a significant part in that process.

<u>The 7 hidden reasons why employees leave organisations</u>

People become dissolutioned with their boss for a variety of reasons, none of which have anything to do with money or monetary rewards. It is a simplistic myth that churn in the workforce is caused by pay relativities. Pay may become a factor in the search for a new job, but that search is not usually initiated because of pay.

What are the factors that cause employees to go looking outside?

i. Loss of trust in my leader – your boss does or says things which mean you no longer trust them.
ii. Lack of coaching – if you don't get regular feedback from your boss, how will you know what they think of you? Employees have that constant unspoken question in their head – "how am I doing?" They need the type of boss who can and will answer it for them.
iii. Lack of growth opportunity – if subordinates can't see how to develop themselves, or where to go next, they will seek that elsewhere. Discussion about your future, and how to develop within the organisation, is a highly retentive conversation.
iv. Lack of recognition – when your boss doesn't thank you for a job well done, or effort made above and beyond the call of duty, you will become demotivated. If this becomes a regular pattern, you will withdraw effort, and begin to look elsewhere. Everyone likes and needs to be appreciated, and yet, in a 2019 UK employee survey, a staggering 62% said that they were never recognised by their boss. 16% of employees in that same survey said that they were on the market, looking for a new job role, because they didn't feel valued.

v. A mismatch of job to person – organisations can be guilty of putting 'square pegs into round holes', and then trying to 'knock the corners off' the employee. Constantly requiring employees to change, rather than allowing them to work at what they do best, is a recipe for labour turnover. Read the work of Marcus Buckingham on this subject, concerning 'playing to people's strengths'.

vi. Expectations not met – organisations can be found guilty of 'promising the earth' during the hiring process, but the reality day to day afterwards can be very different. Don't over-promise when attracting talent, only to then proceed to under deliver.

vii. Poor work-life balance – people have a family, and a life outside the workplace. Seeking to get a blend of life and work which suits the employee will be retentive. If their work rota fits with fetching children from school, they will be very happy with their place of work accommodating that very real need. Putting employees in a situation where they are having difficulty operating as a parent or carer for elderly relatives, will cause them stress and ultimately produce churn.

'Bad Bosses' fail to realise the humanity of their workforce

It stands to reason, that if people feel good at work, their performance will be enhanced. Every employee has extra discretionary effort, which they will give in the right circumstances.

'Bad Bosses', who think that work is purely transactional, fail to realise this potential, and consequently fail to ever realise it. In a recent UK employee survey, some 72% of employees said that they would work hard if they felt appreciated! That is a staggering statistic, and an indictment on leadership.

Warwick Business School, in research work done during 2017, found that employees would be some 12% more productive if they were recognised at work. That is a huge statistical upside for discretionary effort. All the leader needs to do, is to practice praising real outperformance; telling stories to the workforce which celebrate successes and very simply and sincerely learn to say "thank you" where appropriate. This sort of leadership behaviour is not exactly 'rocket science', and yet it appears rare. Leaders need to realise that they can hugely affect the demeanour and happiness of their workforce, by their own behaviour.

Humans are fundamentally social beings, and working in a happy atmosphere, where people are recognised for their achievements, will release dopamine into their bodily system. Giving employees a feel-good 'hit', will enhance productivity. Which leader wouldn't want to tap into that?

What marks out the Good Boss?

This book has set out the top 10 pitfalls of bad bosses, which most irritate followers:-

- Favouritism/Nepotism.
- Indiscretion/Gossiping.
- Claiming the work done by others as your own.
- Being a poor communicator.
- Failing to live the Company values.
- Excessive ego and hubris.
- Not listening to your people.
- Failing to manage people's performance.
- Bullying and sexual harassment.
- Being insensitive/not caring about people.

What then characterises a 'Good Boss', apart from avoiding those pitfalls?

Good leaders connect with people. Their 'door' (even if they work in open plan) is metaphorically always open. This means that they never ignore people who want a few minutes of their time. Effective leaders listen to people, establish working relationships, and show humanity through empathy. If you are approachable as a boss, and a good listener, you will enhance trust between you and your teams. Trust is a vital component in creating a climate of high performance. Authentic bosses genuinely show interest in their people, and take time to understand what motivates them, and 'how they tick'.

Good leaders have competency in what they do, and make decisions about the problems which arise, based on the information that they have at the time. The world is full of data, and it is easy to be paralysed by analysis. The best bosses talk to people, take a wide range of views, read the data, and make a decision. You cannot lead without 'knowing your stuff', but also being willing to take calculated risks. Followers admire sensible risk taking in a leader.

If hubris and ego are loathed by followers, then being humble as a leader is the way to go. Robert Greenleaf wrote his seminal book on the subject of 'Servant Leadership' way back in 1970. However, it very much ties in with the later research work of Jim Collins, which went into his famous book 'Good to Great'. Collins talks about the concept of Level 5 leadership, which he observed in the leaders of so many successful enterprises over the long term. Level 5 leaders exhibited humility and determination as their key characteristics. Humble leaders tend to listen, and are prepared to try new ideas, and ways of tackling challenges. They recognise the contribution that others can bring to any situation. This is a far superior approach to the hubris and ego of the self-centred boss.

Good leaders are fantastic communicators, particularly in the way they address their workforce. They seek to inspire their people on every occasion. Whether they are on stage at a conference, or in small groups or one to one conversations. Their passion, clarity and enthusiasm shine through them, and they are natural story tellers. Before social media, video and technology generally, mankind passed knowledge down the centuries by storytelling. Storytelling remains a very powerful tool for the great boss to utilise. Great communication is the 'rocket fuel' of a high performance business culture.

Good leaders are also role models for others. It is no good, in the 21st century, to simply ask subordinates to do as you say. It is far more powerful, for those questioning observers who watch you, to encourage your people to do as you do. Leaders who are the exemplar of what is required will get better results. Leaders who are effective live by the mantra 'do what you say you will do'. Credibility comes from doing, not just from talking. Leaders need to 'walk the talk'.

Concluding remarks

I hope you have enjoyed reading this book. In many ways, I would have preferred not to have had to write it. The fact is, that there are still a lot of 'Bad Bosses' out there. They are alive and well, and doing some really bad things to their people.

I hope that in highlighting the top 10 pitfalls of leaders, it will enable readers to measure leadership behaviours, and to root these things out of organisations where they are in charge. Don't measure woolly concepts. Ask employees if any of these 10 things are happening?

If you don't currently measure leadership behaviour, then please consider doing so. Never assume that just measuring output and key performance indicators is the whole story. As the words of the song say "it's not what you do, it's the way that you do it". Just think of what your enterprise could achieve in output terms, if your leaders weren't doing things which switched off the discretionary effort of your workforce!

I find it shocking that 62% of the British workforce of today, are never recognised or thanked by their boss, for genuine outperformance. There is no wonder that the nation has a productivity problem. It is not all down to under investment or technology – some of it will be down to human behaviour and how we are managing our people.

Will you become a leader in the vanguard of change? Will you seek to be a fastidious measurer of the behaviour of your leaders? Will you then root out those pitfalls which followers most hate? I trust that you will, and wish you every success in doing so!

SUMMARY POINTS:

- 'Bad Bosses' lack people skills, and have poor Emotional Intelligence.
- People don't leave organisations, they leave bosses.
- 'Bad Bosses' treat people as transactional entities, and not as real people with feelings.
- People are social beings, and work atmosphere affects performance – leaders create the atmosphere – good or bad.
- Good bosses connect with people and show humanity through empathy.
- Good bosses 'know their stuff' and are decisive.
- Good bosses have a servant leader style.
- Good bosses are inspirational storytellers.

YOUR ACTIONS:

- Become a leader who role models what you require.
- Be a leader who routinely measures leadership behaviours as well as key performance indicators. The 'how' matters as much as the 'what'.

Lightning Source UK Ltd.
Milton Keynes UK
UKHW041301110220
358535UK00001B/9

9 781786 236616